Consulting Fees

A Guide for Independent Consultants

www.consultantjournal.com

Consultant Journal

Andréa Coutu, MBA

Copyright information.

Internal book design by Peggy Richardson. Cover Design by Odette Hidalgo.

Library and Archives Canada Cataloguing in Publication Data

Coutu, Andréa . L., 1973-

ISBN# 978-1-927620-00-7

Consulting Fees, A Guide For Independent Consultants : non-fiction/ by Andréa Coutu.

Also issued in digital format.

I. Business & Economics – Consulting II. Title.

Book sales in North America & Internationally:
ConsultantJournal.com/Store

Also by the same author:
- Write Your Business Plan Now
- Discover Your Inner Consultant
- Discover Your Inner Entrepreneur for Moms
- Become a Consultant: How to Make the Leap – a Start-up Course

ConsultantJournal.com
Vancouver, BC, CANADA

Consulting Fees

A Guide For Independent Consultants

By Andréa Coutu, MBA

PRAISE FOR *CONSULTANTJOURNAL.COM*

As a serial entrepreneur, worldwide consultant in screenprinting technologies for 30+ years, and a published author of 42 books on the screenprinting process, I have read a lot of books in my thirst for knowledge. However, Andréa Coutu's Consulting Fees: A Guide for Independent Consultants *is the only one that I have read six times and keep referring as my mentor for setting my fees. It has provided a great many 'Ah ha!' moments. This book is essential reading for even the most successful consultant or those just starting out.*

- Bill Hood, Owner
Bill Hood Consulting

As a seasoned employment attorney, I was seeking an opportunity to expand my practice and expertise in the realm of consulting. Andréa's guide was (and is) an invaluable resource in diversifying my practice. I highly recommend her guide to any professional interested in taking a different direction with his/her career. Her advice on setting up a new practice/strengthening an existing consulting practice, pricing considerations, identification of 'good' clients, and marketing appropriately is concise, clear and simply outstanding.

- Alicia J. Haff, President
Haff Consulting Services, LLC

Consulting Fees: A Guide for Independent Consultants *provided valuable information that assisted me with my educational consulting firm. Even though I had some experience with setting fees for my work, your book gave me additional insight into areas that I hadn't considered. As a result, I have been able to effectively help my clients accomplish their mission and charge a fair and equitable price as well. I would recommend your book to anyone with doubts about establishing financial commitments for their business.*

- Dr. Ethel J. Hasty
President, Mobius Paradigms, LLC

PRAISE FOR *CONSULTING FEES, A GUIDE FOR INDEPENDENT CONSULTANTS*

Simply put, buying this book probably was the best decision that I've made so far for my new consulting business. As the author points out, setting your consulting fee might be the most important strategic business decision you make. The pitfalls of setting fees that are too high seem obvious. However, as the author explains, setting your fee too low can also have all sorts of unintended negative consequences. Setting fees "just right" is very tricky, and the author does a fantastic job of leading you through the process of figuring out how to do that. The book feels more like a conversation or consultation than a book in some respects. She avoids jargon, and provides a great balance of explanation, anecdote, and examples from consultants who have also struggled with the issue of setting fees. It is also very thorough and methodical, with just the right amount of detail to make it useful to a business owner. You neither have to weed through the unnecessary to get critical information, nor are you left with unanswered questions.

- Linda Dunbrack, Owner
Snap Analytical Consulting, LLC

After spending 20 years working at big companies, I finally started my own consulting business. Like all consultants, I wasn't sure how to price my services. But then I found Consulting Fees, *which has been instrumental in helping me setting up the financial side of the business. This book is for the newbie consultant like myself or the Experienced Consultant. It helps think through how your hours, your costs, your expected margin, etc. should be included in each client engagement and in your longer-term business plan. It's a Playbook with How-Tos and a Menu with different options and approaches. It is a must have tool for all business owners.*

- Scott K. Wilder
Reaching SMBs LLC

To all those who ever picked themselves up and carried on, and to those who gave them a little support along the way.

CONTENTS

Section I:
The Basics of Fees

This planet has – or rather had – a problem, which was this: most of the people living on it were unhappy for pretty much of the time. Many solutions were suggested for this problem, but most of these were largely concerned with the movements of small green pieces of paper, which is odd because on the whole it wasn't the small green pieces of paper that were unhappy.

~ Douglas Adams

CHAPTER 1

Knowing Money Matters

As a consultant, you make your living from providing professional advice. And, like any other professional, you need to charge for that work. Otherwise, you won't be able to make a living at it. But, figuring out how much to charge for that advice can be a tricky and sometimes intimidating process.

When I started out as a consultant, I set my fees fairly low. I naively thought that low fees would make me attractive to companies struggling for cash. And I was right. Companies with no money to pay me lined up! Sure, many of them actually did pay me, but several others tried to take advantage of me. They wanted me to go beyond the project scope. They wanted me to accept payments that were long overdue. Or they tried to avoid paying at all.

I learned four things from that experience. (Only four? Well, probably more than four. But four things material to this discussion, anyway!) The first was that I needed to have great contracts and proposals, so that all the terms, conditions, deliverables and measures of completion were ironed out. The second was that I needed to get a deposit on all projects, so that I had some cash flow, commitment and signs of good faith from the other party. The third was that I needed to keep good records, in case I needed to sue a company. (I successfully took two clients to court for unpaid projects – I defended myself and won. Two for two!) Finally, I needed to set my consulting fees so that I signaled my value in the market and deterred bottom feeders.

In fact, by raising my consulting fees, I attracted more "good" clients. Often, the companies that can't (or won't) pay you market rates are the ones who will try to stretch out payment dates, avoid paying, never pay or try to quibble over deliverables. Companies that respect your right to charge professional fees will treat you like a professional.

However, when you decide to charge professional rates for your professional opinion, you can't simply charge $500 an hour and sit back and wait for the money to roll in. You still need to set rates in line with your solution's value in the market. And figuring that out takes time.

If you've got fees on your mind, you're not alone. When I started ConsultantJournal.com in 2006, I had no idea that my blog post on consulting fees would become so well known. Today, it's still the most popular article on the site, bringing thousands of readers each month. As a marketing consultant, though, I shouldn't be surprised. You see, in marketing strategy, we talk about the 4 Ps – product, price, promotion and place (distribution). Well, your consulting fee certainly represents price and it affects how you structure your product – your services – and how you promote, represent and offer your services.

Whether you're setting your fee for the first time or revising your pricing based on a change in your experience, service offering or market position, the process may seem a bit mysterious. You may feel awkward asking other consultants for help. Bringing up money may be culturally taboo, depending on where you live and work. It may involve showing too many of your cards, if you worry that clients will think you're gouging them, pushing them too hard or otherwise using some slight of hand. And tipping your hand may put you at risk of giving your competitors too much information, perhaps so they can price match or undercut you. And if you're feeling like that, imagine how your fellow consultants feel. You're not alone.

When I sat down to write the first version of this book, I focused on helping establish simple models for calculating fees. And the first part of this book still includes those details. But, over the past several years at *Consultant Journal* – not to mention more than 16 years in my own consulting business – I've had a chance to see the complexities in setting fees. Over the years, I have updated and expanded this guide, taking into account the delicate balance of mathematical models, market position, personal preference, client management, cultural and competitive signals and feedback from readers. From a single blog post has emerged this book.

Using *Consulting Fees*, you can learn how to determine your market rate and ask for it with confidence....all without having to talk to your competitors, risk raising your clients' ire or looking uncertain in a professional setting.

Money may be the husk of many things but not the kernel. It brings you food, but not appetite; medicine, but not health; acquaintance, but not friends; servants, but not loyalty; days of joy, but not peace or happiness.

~ Henrik Ibsen

CHAPTER 2

Understanding Fees

When you work as a consultant, you earn your living when people pay you for your professional advice. Perhaps you usually think of that advice in terms of time – or maybe you've already moved on to Solution-Based Fees™. Regardless of how you look at it, your advice may show up as plans, project management, writing, analysis, coaching, selling or any number of activities. Given the wide variety of work you might be doing, you may be wondering how to set your fees.

Most people approach consulting fees from an emotional point of view. They think about how much they'd like to earn and set their fees accordingly. They react to how much their friends or competitors charge by setting a fee that's the same, slightly lower or slightly higher. Others think of their fees as a carrot they can dangle to attract new clients – and clients love low prices, don't they? Still others pick a number that feels good and use that.

But your consulting fee represents a business strategy. Part marketing tool, part financial tool, your consulting fee helps you attract and retain profitable client relationships that will support your economic livelihood and reinforce your brand. Set your fees too low and you'll be working too hard for too little for the wrong clients. Set your fees too high and you'll deter potential clients and end up spinning your wheels. Set them just right (as Goldilocks said) and you'll be poised for success. And all of that will affect your emotions – trust me.

To be a successful consultant, you need to approach your consulting fees as a strategic endeavor. By using the same strategies that big companies use to price their products, you can make sure you set your fees for the right market, clients, competitive environment and more.

Consultant Profile:

Wendy J. Acosta
Acosta & Associates, Inc.
(509) 599 1514
wacasta@msn.com

Q: Tell me about your business.

I work with indigenous people to use their cultural strengths and traditional values to develop resources that build healthy children, healthy families and strong communities. I use my expertise in youth/community development, strength based programs and human systems dynamics to empower hope.

Q: How did you get started?

Being in the right place at the right time. It's actually turned into a spiritual journey with a global vision.

Q: How did you come up with your fees?

Calculating tax liability, expenses and the value of my expertise.

Q: How do you feel about money, revenue and pricing?

It's a cost of doing business. While I would love to be able to do my work for free (and I set my fees so I can afford to donate my time regularly), maintaining certifications, wellness and licensure requires an investment in self.

Q: What advice would you give to other people thinking about their fees?

Give value with every hour you bill, and you will find that other people will gladly pay you for your expertise.

Notes, Thoughts and Questions about this Chapter

Things I want to consider:

Things that occurred to me:

Questions I have:

Money is the root of all evil, and yet it is such a useful root that we cannot get on without it any more than we can without potatoes.

~ Louisa May Alcott

CHAPTER 3

Analyzing Your Situation

Some people contact me, asking where they can get a handout with recommended consulting fees for their industry. But that's not a particularly helpful endeavor. Even if I put together a market survey detailing fees for consultants, it wouldn't really help you in your business.

That's because your business, your market and your skillset are unique. To get an understanding of how that shapes the fees you charge, consider the example of two consultants working in financial services.

Let's say the first is Sally, a 45-year-old financial services consultant and chartered financial analyst who previously worked as a vice-president for an investment banking firm. She works out of New York City serving Fortune 500 clients with multi-million dollar problems that must be solved urgently. And let's call the second consultant Fred, a financial services consultant who previously worked as a bank teller and assistant savings & loans bank manager before moving to a non-profit to work as a credit counselor. He works out of his home in a farming community in Iowa and works directly with farming families to help them with financial planning. Both Sally and

Fred work as financial services consultants, but their specific services, qualifications, skillsets and markets mean that they have very different businesses. And trying to compare their consulting fees would provide absolutely no advantage to either. It comes down to their unique position.

And you're in the same boat. Your unique situation – your experience, qualifications, target market, field, service offering and other details – have a huge impact on the kind of business you run.

Before you get into setting fees, spend some time thinking about your situation. The information you uncover in this exploration will help you set your fees.

What field are you in?

Determine the scope of your business. Identify the kind of consulting you do, along with the industry of your clients. Take note of your geographic marketing area – neighborhood, region or country. For example, you may be a:

- Database integration consultant for small-to-mid-sized businesses in Dallas, Texas

- Management consultant for nursing homes in Delaware

- Beverage consultant for bars and restaurants in Western Australia

- Accessibility consultant for web-based applications for international government

In what field would you put your business?

What services do you provide?

Be specific. Note all services you plan to provide – from the smallest tasks to the most general roles. Group your services under main categories. For example, as a marketing consultant, I provide:

Business Retention & Lead Generation

- Lead management systems

- Generation of contacts, leads, and clients

- Retention of existing clients

- End-to-end lead management

- Sales pipeline analysis

- Development of tools to support lead conversion and business retention

Research, Analysis & Strategic Planning

- Business plan development

- Identifying market opportunities

- Market and sales forecasting

- Triangulation of market data

- Pricing, costing, and financial analysis

- Return on investment calculation

- Strategic analysis

Communications

- Strategic communications planning

- Messaging

- Positioning

- Project management

- Collateral development

- Web management

- Event management

- Online marketing programs

- Direct mail

- Database marketing

- Writing and editing

- Creative concepts

- Art direction

- Vendor management

This is far more complex than just saying I'm a marketing consultant. By breaking my services down, I get a better understanding of the strategic value I provide for clients. In fact, just in listing out those points above, I can see that I've moved away from providing some of those services and that I could provide more detail on others. But having a pretty good idea of my overall offering helps me figure out where to focus my firm's activities.

To set your consulting fees, you need to understand all possible scenarios in which you could be providing consulting. If you think of yourself as an "IT consultant", "event management consultant" or "freelance writer", you'll face challenges in valuing your services. By better understanding how you help clients, you'll be in a better situation to match your fees to the value you create.

Right now, what services do you think you offer? If you haven't started, what services will you offer?

Services I offer:

What goals do you have for your business?

Your business goals will help define your consulting fees. If you're a start-up consultant with little professional experience, you'll need to quickly attract credible, referenceable clients. If you're an established consultant with a long client list, you may be looking to increase profits and cut the costs associated with servicing clients.

Goals I have for my business this year:

In three years:

In five years:

What sort of image do you want?

The image you project will influence (and be influenced by) the fees you charge. If you present yourself as a hired gun known for fast project turnarounds, your "spaghetti Western" heritage may mean clients expect your low overhead to translate to lower rates. And, if you're a veteran consultant to law firms, you may need to have a fee that reflects your serious expertise. Get a good sense of your image before you start thinking about your fees.

What image are you trying to convey?

What would you need to do to be able to keep up that image consistently and legitimately?

Put a dot below to represent your image and positioning. Add your competitors too.

Figure 1: Positioning Map

		Services	
		Low Touch	High touch
Pricing	High	Difficult to justify	Need to deliver on service and marketing
	Low	May work if you have volume or turnaround	Difficult to provide

If you aim to provide low touch service for a high price, you will need to work hard to justify your positioning. However, if you are in a niche field, with few competitors and multiple barriers to entry, you may be able to manage this position. If you aim for high touch services with higher pricing, you will need to work hard to manage customer expectations and your costs. For low touch service and low pricing, you will need to manage your costs and achieve volume through quick turnaround times. If you want to offer high touch services for a low price, you will have to figure out some competitive advantages – perhaps you work from home or have a fantastic, inexpensive team of virtual assistants. Whatever your position, think about what you will need to maintain it.

What's your SWOT (strengths, weaknesses, opportunities, threats) analysis?

A SWOT analysis will help you make sense of your unique strengths and weaknesses, so that you can mitigate threats and create opportunities. What are your strengths? Weaknesses? What opportunities do you have? What threats do you face?

For some reason, doing a SWOT stumps some people. The trouble is that they can't quite figure out the difference between strengths and opportunities and between weaknesses and threats. So here's what I tell them....

Strengths and weaknesses are things within your control. They're related to you or your firm. For example, you might have excellent knowledge of your field or amazing customer relationships. And you may have a weakness when it comes to doing bookkeeping or keeping up with social media. But that's stuff going on with you or your company.

In comparison, opportunities and threats are within your external world. So the demand for green products might be an opportunity for you, while the end of cheap credit might be a threat. You can't really control opportunities and threats – they're outside of you and your firm. See below for a quick summary.

Figure 2: SWOT Analysis

Strengths & Weaknesses	Within your control • employees • technologies • patents • facilities • financial stability • supplier relationships
Opportunities & Threats	Out of your control • economy • competition • law • social and cultural trends

Now try it for your own firm:

Figure 3: SWOT Self-Analysis

	Positive (Helpful)	Negative (Harmful)
Internal	Strengths	Weaknesses
External	Opportunities	Threats

What market share do/will you have?

Your market share will influence the fees you can charge. If you're an unknown, you may need to cut prices to attract clients. But, if you own your market, you might be able to raise fees and risk losing a few clients, in exchange for higher profits.

What I know about the existing market:

Why ask all these questions?

These questions are the same ones marketers use to develop marketing plans. That's because setting prices – or consulting fees – falls under marketing. Without a firm understanding of your own business, you won't be able to figure out how price fits into the marketing mix.

Consultant Profile:

Sylvia Henderson, Springboard Training
E-Mail: Sylvia@SpringboardTraining.com
Web: www.SpringboardTraining.com

Springboard Training is a minority- and woman-owned company based in Olney, MD. Founded by Sylvia Henderson in 2000, Springboard Training serves clients worldwide to help you grow and improve upon your interpersonal communications, positive first impressions, professional behaviors, and mindsets for business success. Products and services include on-site and virtual learning opportunities, physical and electronic information products, and one-on-one and group consulting.

Sylvia Henderson, Implementation Strategist, helps individuals and teams get out of their heads and into action with their ideas, for profit and purpose. Clients call her the "Clarity Queen of Ideas". Using her design thinking process called IMPACT©, Sylvia helps you get clear about, develop strategies for, take action on, and be accountable to your ideas. Sylvia is the author of multiple books including "Hey, That's My Idea!", and hosts a cable TV program on implementing ideas. Turn your dreams into dollars, concepts into cash, and ideas into impact with Sylvia's expertise & experience to guide and encourage you.

Q: How did you get started?

I got "reorganized" out of a technology company in 1999 and decided to do what I did best over the previous 20 years of corporate employment - train, speak, and write focusing on interpersonal communication and other life skills - on my own.

Q: How did you come up with your fees?

At first, guesswork. I know how much I signed for contracts for companies such as Franklin Covey and AMA for courses for my employees when I worked in the corporate world. I set my fees according to those contracts. Fees differ for keynote speaking, one-day training programs, and consulting services. After speaking with my peers in the National Speakers Association and attending workshops on being paid what you're worth, I raised my fees. Yet, as I pursue government contracts, my fees seem to be too high as I have lost several bids with feedback that I am more expensive than my competition. I now am being encouraged, by several friends who are also business colleagues, to charge less by the hour and more by the project results.

Q: How do you feel about money, revenue and pricing?

I like money. I'm in business to make money. While I find personal satisfaction helping other people and seeing that "learning light" flash in their eyes, I need to pay my mortgage, want to buy a nicer car, and have vacation and philanthropic plans that I want to fulfill. I want to price my services fairly, yet set my fees to be indicative of my value. I'm not sure that I am reaching the "right" decision-makers or clients who can pay, and appreciate, my fees without the "nickel-diming" negotiations I keep encountering.

Q: What advice would you give to other people thinking about their fees?

Study the competition to learn the market. Yet, also determine the client and contacts you need who will say "yes" to your services and value in spite of your fees. (Still working on this later advice for myself.)

Notes, Thoughts and Questions about this Chapter

Things I want to consider:

Things that occurred to me:

Questions I have:

The toughest thing about the power of trust is that it's very difficult to build and very easy to destroy. The essence of trust building is to emphasize the similarities between you and the customer.

~ Thomas J. Watson (IBM)

CHAPTER 4

Considering Your Client

Once you've got a sense of your own business, it's time to take stock of your target clients. As a consultant, you can't be all things to all people. Most successful consultants work toward owning a niche. By focusing on a specific kind of client, you can make sure that your fees – and all your marketing strategies – line up with client expectations.

Startup

Startup companies are new firms, known for high potential and high risk. By bootstrapping themselves, startups minimize investment capital and seek high contributions from their workers so they can maximize profits. Although angel investors and venture capital firms sometimes help these companies get off the ground, many start ups are funded by their founders, who rack up personal loans, mortgages and credit card debt.

Start-up businesses tend to be informal, aggressive and entrepreneurial. They're more likely to take a risk on a consultant who lacks formal credentials and conventions, as long as that consultant can deliver results. However, given the bootstrapped nature of startups, you'll face a combination of high expectations, extreme price sensitivity and possible delayed payments. Because founders have such a high stake in these businesses, they tend to manage their money as, well, their money. So they're hesitant to part with cash.

SOHO (Small office, home office)

SOHO companies usually have fewer than 10 employees and many work from home offices. The owners of these companies tend to wear many hats. Because of the size of the company, the owners can still have control over day-to-day operations and many will want to work with you at every step of a project.

Small business

Small businesses have made it past the early days. They're less hungry than startups, but they may have been burned a few times. Expect small businesses to want detailed information and proposals, as well as some handholding. In many cases, the founders are still involved and may want to deal directly with you. Although profit is a key motivator, the owners may see their business as part of a personal ambition or self-actualization.

Mid-sized companies

These companies have been around long enough to make it through ups and downs and to put some structure in place. They tend to be more formal than smaller firms and often have plans, processes and strategies already in place. Although nowhere near as rigid as multinationals, mid-sized companies take a little longer to make moves and often need to go through several hoops before they will make a decision.

Major companies and multinationals

Whether they are part of the Fortune 500 or not, major companies have structure, power and influence. Because many are publicly traded, they may need to seek board approval or meet other protocols before hiring you. In many cases, these companies have bidding and requests for proposals. However, sometimes they can be flexible and nimble in hiring a consultant – it just depends. In some cases, if you are successful with one branch or location of the firm, you may be able to be hired to do work elsewhere.

Government clients

The government sector includes everything from small townships to federal governments. Like major corporations, government clients tend to be bogged down in protocol, requests for proposals and other structure. However, they offer consultants an opportunity to influence the way government works. In many cases, government clients offer big budget, long-term consulting opportunities, where you can have the opportunity to make a contribution over the span of months or years. Although some consultants think a government client means an opportunity to jack up prices and draw out delivery dates, the reality is that most governments are price sensitive.

Non-profit clients

Struck by the power of helping a good cause, consultants often like to give non-profits a break by charging less. However, instead of charging less, why not consider quoting your regular rate and donating the money back? You'll receive a tax break, the non-profit can show its board higher donations and the value of your work will be better recognized.

Clients I will pursue: (check those that apply)

_   A - Startup

_   B - SOHO (Small office, home office)

_   C - Small business

_   D - Mid-sized companies

_   E - Major companies and multinationals

_   F - Government clients

_   G - Non-profit clients

Figure 4: Characteristics of these clients:

Client Type	Similarities	Differences
A		
B		
C		
D		
E		
F		
G		

Evaluating your environment

Industry

The industry in which you work will put some parameters around the fees you can charge. For example, in the editing field, different kinds of editors earn different kinds of fees. For example, an editor of poetry books may only be able to charge $15 an hour, whereas an experienced, specialized technical editor for the aerospace industry may be able to command more than $150 an hour.

Competition

To some degree, your competition will dictate what you can charge. If you undercut your competitors, clients may think you're inferior. Of course, if you are starting out, have no track record, and generally lack the same qualifications, you should seek to charge at the lower end of fair market value. If you deliver the same services and results as your competitors, you will face an uphill battle in charging more. However, if you can determine how to add value, differentiate your services and stand out from the crowd, you may be able to raise your fees above those of the competition.

Your background

In setting your fees, take some time to think about your qualifications and services. As noted above, you should think about how you compare to the competition, then seek to carve out a niche. If you can position yourself as a high quality, well-qualified, specialized player, you can charge higher fees. If you're new to the game, you may need to start your fees a little lower. However, be cautious about using low fees as a way to attract clients. Price-sensitive clients tend not to stick around when you need to raise your fees. Instead, price according to how you've positioned yourself in the market.

Regulations

In certain industries, fields and professions, you may face regulations from government or professional bodies. For example, real estate agents and lawyers need to work within regulatory environments. Make sure you understand any regulations you face. Sometimes, your fees may be set or limited by government or professional associations.

My understanding of the business environment:

Industry

My industry:

Trends:

Problems:

Other information I have gathered:

Competition

General competitive environment:

Major competitors for my business:

Their likely responses to my firm:

Your background

My business's competencies and positioning:

Regulations

Government and policy changes:

Professional:

Legal:

Environmental:

Other:

Consultant Profile:

Morgaine O'Herne, Morohe Design and Consulting
morgainebrigid@gmail.com.
Website: http://morohe.com
Blog: http://morgainebrigid.blogspot.com

Q: How did you get started?

I began by designing my own ecommerce site years ago, and realized I found web design fascinating. For many years thereafter I wasn't able to devote much time to honing my skills because I was stuck in a series of dead-end foodservice jobs and failed businesses. Recently my health forced me to quit both and I'm devoting my time to learning web design.

Q: How did you come up with your fees?

My fees right now are the minimum suggested on the site I mostly look for jobs on — Elance — because I really want the opportunity to get established. I know my time is worth more, but I also know I need to prove it. I'd rather be underpaid for a job I like than be totally screwed by the types of jobs I've been in (retail and food service)

Q: How do you feel about money, revenue and pricing?

I feel that all the conventional jobs I've ever had have underpaid and overused me, and are the major cause of my health problems now. I know I could easily be taken advantage of as a consultant too, but don't know how else to establish myself other than undercutting those who are already established. I don't know for sure whether I'm charging low because I think that's the only way in, or because I have self-esteem values. Talking about money frightens me. I'm afraid people will reject me if I ask too much, and I'm afraid they'll think my work's no good if I charge too little.

Notes, Thoughts and Questions about this Chapter
Things I want to consider:

Things that occurred to me:

Questions I have:

If money is your hope for independence you will never have it. The only real security that a man will have in this world is a reserve of knowledge, experience, and ability.

~ Henry Ford

CHAPTER 5

Setting Your Fees

Once you've taken steps to evaluate the unique situation you face as a consultant, you're ready to begin the process of setting your fees. Although most people think of fees as finance-oriented, price is actually one of the four P's of marketing.

Far from being a mere estimation of your value, your fee serves as a valuable marketing tool. Set low, it may help you achieve rapid market penetration. Set high, it may position you as a highly skilled consultant. However, set too low, it may make your services appear inferior. Set too high, it may make you look arrogant. Pricing is both psychological and financial in nature.

When you set your fees, you also make a decision about how you approach the market. If you have rare and valuable services, you may be able to command a high fee, allowing you to skim the market before eventually lowering your prices and going after the mainstream. However, if you work in an intensely competitive field, you may need to start with lower prices, so that you can grab market share.

Moreover, you need to consider existing price points for your services. If other consultants in your field have already set the bar, you need to determine whether you should price above or below them. If you're new to the market, you may need to price below the average, until you establish a client list. But you still need to choose a fee that's in line with the rest of the market, or you'll look inferior and you'll have trouble ever raising your rates later. Likewise, if you offer premium skills and services, you may want to price above the average, but within the limits of what is generally considered reasonable.

That being said, it's often difficult to figure out the going rate for consulting services in your field. Most consultants are unwilling to tell their competitors what they charge, for fear of being underbid. And clients aren't about to tell you how much they pay your competitors. Although some professional and trade associations collect data on consulting fees, it's often difficult to get realistic information about fees. Most importantly, in many countries, such as the United States and Canada, discussions about price may fall under "price fixing" law.

Given those challenges, I suggest using one of the following strategies to set your fees:

- Double or triple your hourly wage

- Cost- and profit-based analysis

- Charging the going rate

- Charging by the project

- Solution-Based Fee™ pricing (this is an advanced step, discussed later in this book)

These are simply suggested models and not the de facto standard for any particular industry. As you'll see, your own situation will influence your approach

Double/triple your hourly wage

To set fees, some consultants simply take the hourly wage (plus benefits) that they would earn when working for someone else and then double or triple it. If you're doing this, you'll probably find that tripling your hourly wage is the best move. Some consultants choose a triple rate because of what they call the rule of thirds -- one third goes to your real wage, one third to expenses, and one third to administration, low utilization and bad debt.

Consider a scenario where you would make $60,000 a year plus $15,000 in benefits at a full-time job, where you take four weeks off a year.

($60,000 salary + $15,000 benefits) / (48 weeks * 40 hours) = $75,000

$75,000 / 1920 = $39.06

$39.06 x 2 = 78.12, rounded up to $80 per hour

Or $39.06 x 3 = $117.18, rounded to $120 per hour.

Of course, this assumes you use an hourly rate for your consulting services. Many people work out an hourly rate, but actually charge by the half-day, day, project or another arrangement.

Cost- and profit-based analysis

This strategy involves several steps:

Calculating working days

In this calculation, you base your charges on working days per year.

52 weeks in a year

Say you allow six weeks for vacation, stat holidays and sick time.

= 46 weeks

46 weeks x 40 hours = 1840 hours a year

Determining your billable hours

As noted above, you have 1840 working hours available each year. However, what percent of your time will be spent on work that brings in money, as opposed to work that helps you find clients but for which you aren't actually paid?

Start with 100% possible hours:

- 20% spent on administration, running errands, paperwork, etc

- 20% spent on marketing, networking events, website management, etc

- 10% spent on other non-billable work

Therefore, 50% spent actually working for pay.

1840 hours x 50% utilization rate = 920 billable hours

Considering bad debt rate

Despite your best intentions, not all your clients will pay you. Some will take weeks or months to pay, but a small percentage will never pay the bill. So consider this in setting your fees.

Let's say one in 20 clients is a deadbeat. Now, keep in mind that most people will pay you. I've rarely run into problems with clients, because I use solid contracts and get deposits up front. But, to give yourself a little breathing room, let's say you do have that occasional client who runs into trouble – not even necessarily because they're a bad guy, but because they ran into their own financial trouble. So, if one in 20 people fails to pay, you need to account for the five percent of hours you work without getting paid. We'll say you collect on 95 percent of the hours you work.

Collection rate: 95%

920 hours x 95% = 874 hours

Figuring out rate of pay

In this step, we take a good look at how much you would make if you were working at a job. Now, some people will tell you that you should only be considering the value you're bringing to the client and the rate they're willing to pay. But most people do realistically have the opportunity to do their work as a job for an employer. And what the employer is willing to offer up is already a strong market signal. It's an indication of what the market is willing to bear for your services. And it's also an indication of the opportunity cost you fact in working as a consultant instead, if you're taking up consulting as a full-time endeavour. If you would otherwise make $50,000 or $100,000 a year doing this for an employer, it makes sense to consider that when you're setting your rate. You can, of course, go up or down from there. But it's worth reviewing. Just make sure you continue through with the calculations here, because, as someone who is self employed, you can't just take your old hourly rate and use that. You most likely need to cover expenses – even things as simple as your desk or Internet fees.

So...how much would you earn if you were paid a salary at a company? Let's use $60,000 a year as an example and assume you have good benefits, worth $15,000 per year.

$60,000 base salary + $15,000 in benefits = $75,000 salary.

Your total compensation divided by the hours you can bill in a year will give us a guideline for your hourly rate. (Remember, those billable hours reflect your total working time in the year, minus administrative work, all adjusted for bad debt.)

Compensation/billable hours = hourly consulting fee

$75,000 salary / 874 billable hours = $85.81.

So, now, your hourly rate is worth just about $86 an hour. But you still have some costs to cover.

Working out overhead rates

If you've got the kind of consulting business that entails pure profit, you might not have to worry about overhead. But most consultants need to allow for:

- rent or mortgage interest
- utilities
- maintenance and upkeep
- property taxes
- Internet
- telephone
- cell phone
- Internet connection
- laptop or desktop computer
- shipping and postage
- printer toner/ink
- paper
- stationery
- accounting (if you don't do your own)

- legal services (in some cases)

- office furniture — desk, chair, shelves, bookcase, filing cabinet, lighting, etc.

- business licenses and permits

- insurance — health, life, disability, liability, etc

- car — insurance, maintenance, gas, lease

- advertising and marketing

- subscriptions

- professional associations

- meals and entertainment for professional purposes

- continuing education

- professional meetings, conferences and tradeshows

- cleaning supplies and cleaning services

- other

To figure out how much this overhead costs you per hour, divide the total cost of your overhead by your billable hours. We'll use $5,000 as your overhead in this example:

$5,000 overhead / 874 hours = $5.72

Now let's add that overhead to the hourly rate we calculated above:

$5.72 overhead + $85.81 fee = $91.53 fee

So now we've established an hourly rate that covers all your costs. But what about profit?

Profit margins

As a consultant, you're taking a risk and running a business. So it's reasonable to expect a profit margin on your fees. Consultants usually mark up their fees by ten percent to 33 percent. Let's use 25 percent.

$91.53 + 25% mark up = $114.41

Since consultants tend to round to the nearest $5, our example results in $115 per hour rate. Incidentally, it's worth noting that this is about three times the hourly wage we used at the start.

Charging the going rate

Sometimes it's simple enough to just charge what everyone else charges for consulting. It comes down to what the market will bear and what your competitors are doing. If you fall in line by charging the same as everyone else, you're signaling that you're a worthy (qualified) consultant who plays fairly. You're also making sure you get the base line rate for consulting in your market. Depending on whether you think you're more or less valuable or experienced than your competitors, you may want to shift your fees up or down by 10 percent. Really, though, the unique solution your business provides and the kinds of clients you target are going to influence your rate. Moreover, once you've been running your business for a while, you may want to position your business so that you can command premium rates – charging the same as everyone else may not work with your long term strategy for differentiation. But, if you do stick with what everyone else charges, no one can fault you for being overpriced, so it can be a place of comfort for now.

Fixed project bids

Some consultants set their rates by the project. They estimate the number of hours they expect to spend on a project, and then multiply by their hourly rate. For example, let's say you build websites. If it takes 20 hours to build a website, you might quote $2,300. On the other hand, you may simply charge a fixed rate for certain projects. A public relations consultant might charge $1,500 for a custom news release and personalized distribution of the release, regardless of how long it takes. A lawyer may charge $750 for basic incorporation, knowing that it usually takes two to three hours to work through the paperwork. A graphic designer may charge $500 to $1,200 for a custom logo, depending on the number of revisions the client needs. In these cases, the consultants have come up with an idea of how long it takes to do a project and the value they provide to the client. Some may tell the client how long they expect to spend on the project and others may just charge a flat rate. A flat rate can work well if you're effiicient and productive, but you may end up eating your quote if you underestimate the time involved. You might be okay with doing that once in a while, if knowing

the final amount pays off for you in other ways –
or if you find you usually finish the project quickly.

Cost-plus pricing

In a cost-plus-fee structure, you simply charge for
your costs plus a profit margin.

Price = (fixed costs) + (variable costs * unit) * markup

For example, let's say you are a software
implementation consultant. When you install five
licenses of office software in an eight-day period, you
face costs of $2800 in overhead and $500 for software
licenses.

Your total costs are thus $3300.

You then charge a mark-up of 33 percent or $990.
So, in this cost plus pricing scenario, you would charge
$4290, plus any applicable taxes.

Although some people love cost-plus pricing for
its simplicity, the approach may be better suited to
products and to consultants who are certain of the
market rate for their wages. If you aren't already
certain of how much to charge for your services and
of what business costs you need to cover, it won't
do you much good to simply tack a mark-up on to
your fees. Moreover, if you base your fees merely
on the cost of performing your services, you do a
disservice to the value you generate for your clients.
Solution-based pricing may be the better way to go.

Per diem (daily) rates

To set a daily rate, simply multiply the hours you work in a day by your hourly rate:

Hours * hourly rate = per diem rate

For example:

8 hours * $80 hourly rate = $640 per day

Some consultants discount this rate because they see efficiencies in being paid for eight hours of work. Others feel that their basic consulting rate covers these efficiencies already. This is really a personal decision, because it depends on how much administrative time you spend on each account.

Special assessments

We all have clients with whom we'd rather not work. Some of the reasons for this include:

- Boring work

- Too much handholding

- Long, inefficient meetings, phone calls or emails

- Repeated last-minute requests

- Personality conflicts

When you're faced with clients and situations like those above, you have three choices. You can "fire" your client, work to solve the situation, or charge a premium for your services. If you're keen to retain the client and you've tried everything you can think of, raise your fees for this client. Think of it as an annoyance tax.

Performance-based fees

Some clients offer consultants a share of future revenue, profits or commissions, pushing the consultant to a pay for performance model. Others offer the client a commission. Still others offer pay based on the results of the consultant's work. Consulting fees based on performance pose several risks. For example, the company's performance in other areas may affect the area in which you are measured. It may take months or more to see the results of the work, meaning that the consultant will not see any revenue for a long period, effectively giving the company an interest-free loan.

And can you trust the client? The company may not cooperate with you in implementing your full recommendations, compromising your ability to reach the potential you projected. Moreover, you may have a hard time checking to see whether the client has manipulated results. Can you be sure that your results are being reported accurately? Most importantly, you shift the focus from high quality planning to short-term gains. If you essentially become a partner by sharing in the client's risk, you may lose your objectivity. At the very least, seek a base rate plus performance pay or share of ownership. Sticking to contingency and performance-based fees opens a can of worms.

Long-term assignments

When faced with the prospect of a long-term contract, it makes sense to discount your rate. Because of the efficiencies of working for a single client for much of your time, you actually save money. Having already secured the client, you won't need to invest as much in marketing and sales activities and you won't have the risk of ongoing downtime. It's fair to discount your rate.

However, don't be tempted to dramatically reduce your rate. Some clients will pressure you to accept ten percent above the hourly salary of their employees. If you are a consultant, you are not an employee. You're someone with a business of your own — and you need to account for your personal and financial risks. Some clients think that offering 10 or 15 percent above an hourly wage should cover this risk. But, when you consider vacation, sick time, retirement benefits, employment insurance, health insurance and the multitude of business costs, this really isn't a premium at all. So, try to strike a balance between recognizing the benefits of a long-term assignment and mitigating the risks of self-employment. One-third off your typical consulting rate may work out.

Some companies try to classify contract employees as consultants, with the hope that they can avoid certain payroll taxes. Check with your government authorities – such as the US Internal Revenue Service

– for help in distinguishing between contract work and self-employment.

If you accept a long-term assignment, do keep up your marketing and networking. When the job ends, you don't want your cash flow to flat line.

Travel time

What do you charge for travel time? When you need to go out of town to see clients, you need to consider your fees for travel time. Consider these points:

- What will the market bear? A senior engineering consultant may be in better position to negotiate than a junior freelance writer.

- What is your competition doing? If everyone in your field charges 50% for travel time, you may not be able to break away without being punished by competitors (or sending clients to your lower-priced competitors).

- What's your relationship with the client like? If you're trying to win a new client, you might be a little more flexible than usual. In comparison, you might be willing to cut a long-time client a deal.

- Can you do work for the client while you're traveling? If you can do other work for the client while you're in transit, you can point this out, putting yourself in a better position to negotiate for full pay.

- Can you do work for other clients? Accepting 50% or 75% for travel time might not be so bad if you can bill other clients for time you spend working on the plane, at the airport, or in restaurants.

- What's the minimum you'll accept? Always go into negotiations knowing the very minimum you're willing to accept. That way, you'll know when to walk away – and when you're getting more than you bargained for.

Thoughts about setting fees

I've used several methods to set my consulting fees over the years. When I first started out, I just charged the rate everyone else at my level was charging. It seemed fair enough and it saved me some headaches. I generally used that method to set my consulting fees for the first six months or so.

However, not long after I became a consultant, I realized that my business was different. I wasn't offering the same services as all the other people. In fact, the feedback I got suggested that I was offering better value and more innovative services. Around the same time, I got some calls from headhunters who wanted me to interview at various companies. I asked them about my prospective salary...then used that information to calculate my rate based on double what I'd be making at a company.

To set my consulting fees, I simply charged a multiple of my salaried rate for the next couple of years. I typically used that rate to charge by the project. Occasionally, my clients told me what they could afford to pay me and I told them what I could deliver at that rate! I still sometimes do that, since I respect that we all have budgets; I propose a solution that takes budget into account, but that doesn't mean someone with $2,500 gets the same solution as someone with $25,000.

A few years ago, I started using another model to benchmark my quotes. I worked out a multiple of what my hourly rate at a "real" job would be. Then I researched what other consultants charged for similar or related services. I used a spreadsheet to come up with a detailed pricing model that included working days, billable hours, rate of pay, overhead and the like. Finally, I did an average of the three figures. Surprisingly enough, the three figures were pretty much in the same ballpark anyway.

Nowadays, I've moved to Solution-Based Fees. This means I pay more attention to the whole solution I offer to my clients and base the fees accordingly. For most people, being able to do that takes experience, confidence and market power. Although some gurus may tell you anyone can start charging fees based on the value of your solution, markets (and buyers) are rational. If you're going to move to those sorts of fees, you need to package your business a certain way.

And that means you need to think strategically and possibly change the way you do business. You still need to pay attention to the competitive environment. And you need to have a certain emotional readiness too. That's why I've saved the discussion on Solution-Based Fees for later in this book.

Coming up with your consulting fee for the first time may seem daunting. However, once you've found a strategy in which you really believe, you'll be good to go. You may want to revisit your decision from time to time, taking into account your experience, client feedback and even your competitors' activities. Eventually, if you're ready, you can move to Solution-Based Fees. That's where the real staying power for your business will come to be.

Consultant Profile:
Senior Consultant, Organizational Development Consulting

(Prefers to remain anonymous)

Q: Tell me about your business.

Largely HR- and organizational development-related consulting with government, not for profit organizations and some private businesses. Most of the work comes in the door from former clients or word of mouth, and some from formal tendering processes. I am a sole trader but work mainly under the umbrella of a small but well established consulting company.

Q: How did you get started?

I was invited to join the small consulting company as a sub contractor after I left the public service after 30 years in various senior public service positions. Initially I was introduced to clients and work by the principal of the company, and this still happens, but I am steadily building my own client base. I have developed a few "bread and butter" specialty products and have captured a significant proportion of the local market for these. There are enormous benefits in working with other experienced consultants and I know I have been lucky to have "trainer wheels" when I first started. We see many lone consultants trying to build a business from home but it is hard and the casualty rate is high.

Q: How did you come up with your fees?

The company had an existing policy about consultant's daily and hourly rates which I use as a starting point for my quotations. The rates are at the upper end of the local scale but our business model is based on quality products, high levels of service customisation, highly experienced consultants and a deep knowledge of our clients. Very occasionally I reduce the rate but only if I am doing the work for a worthy cause or struggling organisation. If I do that, I let the client know that I am doing the job at a cut rate and why.

Q: How do you feel about money, revenue and pricing?

Initially, I underquoted as I was embarrassed to ask for money, but after seriously underquoting on a major job I am much more realistic and confident about quoting and now have few inhibitions about it. I am also much more realistic about the amount of invisible work that you have to do which you cannot usually charge for — such as preparing proposals, preparing materials, and all the administrative minutiae related to the work. I would walk away from a job if the client was not willing to pay the fees, but that has never happened.

Our charges are almost never an issue for our clients, who are generally from large organizations that are much more interested in quality and results than they are about the cost. Value for money is a big issue for our clients, but the overall cost is generally not. We also have the benefit of a very strong reputation in our city and so people are confident about using us, and have a pretty good idea about what it will cost before they ask us to do work for them.

Q: What advice would you give to other people thinking about their fees?

There is no doubt that how the client values you is, in part, shaped by how you value yourself. Your fee schedule will also to some extent determine where you sit in the market and in the hierarchy. So I would advise budding consultants to set their price at the level that they want it to be for the future. In other words, don't try to compete on the basis of cost and then raise the price later. Compete on the basis of quality. If you set your rates too low, it is hard to raise them in the future. If you feel that the client is concerned with the cost, offer an additional service for nothing, or reduce the scale of the service but don't alter the rationale behind the original quote (such as your daily or hourly rate).

Usually the client wants a justification for the quotation, especially where there is a competitive tendering process. I use daily rate and hourly rate, and for training I often use a per capita amount. On top of this all costs are added – such as materials and other expenses. It is more complex if the task is open ended. In this case I usually advise the client to limit their investment to one or two "stages" of the project, and when these are completed, I put up another proposal and quotation for the next stages. This gives you and the client exit points, and the client confidence that they are not looking at a bottomless pit of expenditure.

Finally, it is really, really important that proposals and quotations contain clear outcomes, and that these are signed off. Agreeing on a price is important, but equally important is an agreement about what the client is actually paying for.

Notes, Thoughts and Questions about this Chapter

Things I want to consider:

Things that occurred to me:

Questions I have:

Everything is negotiable. Whether or not the negotiation is easy is another thing.

~ Carrie Fisher

CHAPTER 6

Navigating and Negotiating

Clients and their sticky situations

Once you set your fees, you're on to client management. Just as you have your own reactions to the fee-setting process, so too do your prospects and clients. Some may want to negotiate a bit off the top, whereas others may expect you to work for free. Yes, free. But don't do that – read on.

Working for free

Over the course of your consulting career, you may be approached by prospective clients who want you to work for free. Some of the tactics these people use include:

- Inviting you to prepare "sample" business plans, articles, whitepapers, analyses and reports that address their business issues

- Calling you, giving details of their problem, and then demanding that you give examples of how you would solve their problems, so that they "can see what you're like to worth with"

- Asking you to come for a free lunch to discuss your ideas for doing work for them

- Holding an interview, where they proceed to pick your brain for tips on solving their business problems

- Emphasizing that they're a startup or small business with no funds to pay you

- Suggesting that you don't have the requisite skills to do a paid job, but that they'll consider hiring you once you've done some work during a test period

- Offering to promote your name to their Very Important People so that you gain more credibility

Don't work for free. If you work for free, people will think you're hungry for work and that you don't have enough paying clients. As a result, they will discount your opinions and be unable to see you as a true expert. In fact, in many cases, once they have implemented your ideas, many of these companies will move to an "established" consultant who charges big fees. And others will just keep moving to one consultant from another, in search of more free advice. If they indicate at the outset that they aren't willing to pay for your time, they probably won't ever see your time as valuable. They want a deal or free advice and they're likely to stick with that opinion.

Working on spec

Sometimes, new clients will ask you to work on spec. "Spec work" is short for "speculative work". The client wants you to complete work, without promise for pay or a contract. They claim they will pay you if they like your work. However, if they don't like your work, you have given up time and resources for free. In fact, even if they like your work, they may refuse to pay you, offer a lowball price, or walk away with your design and take months to pay.

Many consultants think it makes sense for a client to "try before they buy". However, spec work means that the client doesn't think enough of you, your client list, your past successes or even your consulting field to offer you a contract. If they see you that way now, doing work for free will often do little to change that.

In most cases, the client has asked you and several other consultants to work on spec. They may think this is a great way to get several different perspectives. However, they aren't allowing you the time to build a relationship, get to know their business or fully understand their problems. They are trying to force quick advice from you.

Without a full understanding of a client's situation, consultants have no choice but to go with "big bang" solutions. Slick proposals, attention-grabbing ideas and dress up ideas take precedence. True consulting falls to the wayside.

By working on spec, you imply that you are someone who will work for free. Once a client knows you will work for free, they have no incentive to ever pay you what you're worth. And your competitors, colleagues, and prospective clients will have no reason to see you as a true professional. How seriously do you think others will take you once they find out you do work for free?

Moreover, when you do work for free, you have to abandon your ethics. Instead of putting forth what you know to be right for the client, you have to produce what the client will buy. However, what if the best advice for the client conflicts with what's best for them?

Finally, if you're starting out as a consultant, you have probably have limited resources and cash flow. What makes the client's business more deserving of charity than yours? Focus on work that pays. Working on spec usually means you end up with no pay or a lowball offer.

Avoiding free first sessions

Some consultants offer their first session for free. This is an odd move, since it signals that your very first meeting has no value. In fact, that very first meeting is critical to the success of your planning for the client and in establishing a strong plan for helping them. If you signal that the meeting has zero value, what does this tell the client? And how committed are you to listening to their needs, as opposed to hoping to convert them to a sale?

Of course, if you're looking at doing high value consulting and building a long-term relationship, it may make sense to meet the prospective client. But make sure you're "meeting" with them and not "consulting" or "coaching" them for free. Keep the focus on a discussion of what they're looking for and what your services are. Avoid telling them how to solve their problem or trying to wow them with your analysis. There's no need for them to buy if they can simply get you to spill your story for a cup of coffee. Your "free" consulting may solve enough of the problem to leave nothing but implementation, which the client or a low-paid employee or contractor may then do.

In fact, if you provide an initial session for free, the client will see you as a source of future free information. And if you're caught up in providing free consulting, it means your sales and marketing process has a major gap. You're still needing to prove your value. So the problem isn't with the free session – it's with what you're doing before you get to that point.

Your goal should be to remove risks from your sales process. Free doesn't pay the bills. Free often wastes your precious time. Ideally, you've triaged your clients before you've met with them. Moreover, many people offer a first meeting for free without regard for the conversion rate. If people are at the "tire kicking" stage, they may take advantage of the free session without ever intending to go forward. Some may be shopping around for as many free sessions as they can find.

To help with this process, it helps to develop a sales and marketing pipeline. As part of that, you should build out a qualification process that helps you identify where buyers are in the cycle. You need to discover where buyers are in the cycle, establish trust, understand their problem, diagnose their needs and identify the pains involved in not solving that problem. When a prospective client is motivated by pain and can envision a solution to that pain, they are much more likely to make a move. However, you need to make sure they have the power and authority to make that change. You need to find out who the buyer is, what key influencers they have, and whether they have the means to buy. For example, a prospective client may be very clear that they need a new website, but if they only have a budget of $1,000 and the decision has to be shopped around to an internal committee before their boss who has the final say, you need to change who you're talking to and determine what you can deliver for that budget, if you can even do so.

In your sales and marketing pipeline, you have people who've never heard of you and may not even know they have much of a problem. At the other end, you have clients who are raving fans who come back for more and encourage their trusted contacts to turn to you for help. But there's a big difference in the relationship between someone who doesn't know who you are and someone who thinks you're brilliant.

Figure 5: Big Black Box Marketing – don't do this!

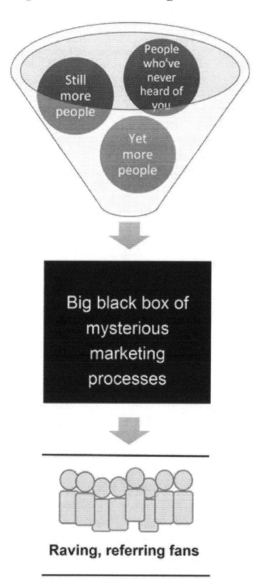

If your marketing process looks like the one in *Figure 5: Big Black Box Marketing*, you're missing some really important pieces along the way.

Really, you need to create a process where you're building relationships with people, so that they move along a pipeline, going through the various stages as needs and trust allow.

This pipeline includes stages. At first, there are people who have never heard of you. Then people you suspect might be need your services. Then those who seem very likely and have passed some initial criteria – you've prospected these, swishing them around in your gold pan as you mine for a find. Leads have an identifiable need, power to buy, authority to buy and so on. Take a look at how this flows in *Figure 6: A few stages in the sales and marketing pipeline*.

If you haven't figured out where a potential client is in this pipeline, it makes no sense to go for an initial meeting. You need to qualify your lead before you move to a meeting.

Figure 6: A few stages in the sales and marketing pipeline

The Larger World

Contact — Someone you know exists

Suspect — Someone you think might need your help / services

Prospect — Someone who has indicated they need help

Lead — Someone who can buy and who suits your offering

Client — Someone who's climbed on board

Champion — Raving, referring fan of you, your company & offer

Underlying marketing tools, strategies and processes

Qualifying leads

People will move along in the pipeline if you've established credibility, built trust, stimulated the pains they are having and given them hope for something better. You can do this by offering marketing tools, such as a website, brochures, articles, blog posts, newsletter, information sessions, workshops, courses and so on – and perhaps even generate revenue from some of those.

If you do get to the point where you're going to meet with a potential client, try to have already communicated who you are, what you do, what problems you solve and who you work with. Educate them through your website, email and marketing materials before you actually need to meet them. And take the time to qualify the potential client, so that you are working with a strong lead, not just someone who wants to kick your tires.

Qualifying a client means working with the client to explore their problems, their current means of addressing the problems, the budget they have and their fit with your offering. If you can tell from the get-go that the clients' processes, branding and relationship skills clash with your approach and values, you've just taken an important step in qualifying the client – in fact, that client shouldn't qualify to work with you, if you are interested in doing your best work. But, if exploring the client's needs starts to get both of you excited about doing the work, they've got a workable budget, you can see how you could help them solve an important problem and you understand their buying process, the client probably makes the cut.

Questions to help qualify leads

Every time I hear the word qualify, I think of an old video game. Back when people still went to arcades, there was a game called Pole Position by Atari and Namco. And every time I walked by, a the arcade box would call out, "Prepare to qualify." Then the game would go beep, beep, booooooooop! And the engines would roar. Well, playing that game is not unlike working with clients. In Pole Position, you had to take control by sitting in the driver's seat, popping a quarter in the machine, choosing a track and setting the difficulty level. Then you had to wait, prepare for the race, think of your strategy, and shift into position when the count-down ended. From there, you had to jockey your position, moving around other drivers and keeping your focus on the finish line, without losing site of other obstacles that might appear before you. In the same way, you need to think through your approach with the client, understand the course you're on, navigate issues that pop up, and navigate around your competitors, never losing sight of the compelling offer you need to make to get to the next round. So think through the course before you and take some time to ask the client questions too.

Points to ponder

What problems does the client have?

Does your business have the ability to solve these problems?

Is there a budget for this project?

Can the company afford not to take on this project?

What would happen if the company didn't take on your project?

What are the dates and milestones for key decisions?

What is this customer's market position?

What's this prospect's financial situation?

Does the prospect understand the value of your solution?

Does this prospect seem similar to others who have bought from you?

Who has the power to make a purchase decision?

Who has the power to approve the budget for this purchase?

Who will influence decision makers for this project?

How does this company make purchase decisions?

What needs to happen before this project is approved by the top decision maker?

And so on.

You may find it helpful to put together a lead qualification sheet. Simply take the questions listed above or any you find relevant and list them out. You can do this in your word process, contact management software or even a good ol' fashioned piece of paper. If you find that you are missing answers to your questions, try to work with the potential client to learn more. In some cases, you may need to set up a meeting with someone else in their organization, especially if the person with whom you are dealing does not really have the authority to approve the budget or make the purchase decision.

Meeting with the potential client

You may or may not charge clients for an initial meeting – some people screen clients over the phone first and charge for a discovery session. If you do meet in person first, limit the free session to identifying some of the client's problems – not all of them, but some of them. This helps you to define the project and other projects – it's a research process. Meet with clients for about 30 minutes to see if there's a fit for needs, services, personality, timeline and budget.

Focus on open-ended questions that encourage the client to give you details. In response, note that you have solutions for their problems and that, by working with you, they can solve these problems. Note that your services can help them address and solve their problems. But keep your boundaries firm and clear – you charge for consulting and this is your business. Once you go over the boundary from identifying problems and explaining a solution, you're working for free. And once clients know your solution, they can shop around for a better price…whether that's in New York City, Birmingham, Vancouver or Bangalore.

Charging for diagnosis

If reviewing the client's problems is a complex and valuable process, you should be charging for it. A quick diagnosis that explains the problems and notes the pains left from not solving them might be free – and that's because you're simply restating what the client told you. But if you're looking at problems in depth, going over potential solutions and recommending a particular solution, you should be doing so for pay.

Better alternatives to free sessions

If you want to get in front of people and give away information, it makes sense to cast a wider net – when you meet one on one, you're only meeting with one client. Instead go with a public seminar on getting started on the route to fitness – or on choosing a personal trainer. Better yet, offer the session for a fee through a community centre, continuing education venue or other organization. Providing information helps establish your expert status and positions you to secure a relationship with a prospective client.

If you have a coaching model, you could consider offering an additional service when they commit to several sessions or certain services. This encourages a longer, more profitable commitment.

You might also offer an incentive when people sign up by a certain date. Knowing you can count on a certain amount of revenue reduces your marketing costs and gets people in the door. By setting a firm date, you encourage conversion.

You can also look at ways to serve the needs of people who are looking for free information. Through blogs, ebooks, articles and handouts, you can help educate and persuade potential clients. When they're ready, you can guide them through your qualification process and determine whether there's a fit. But using information tools at the outset can help you provide basic information without getting bogged down in helping people who are still in the early information-gathering stages of the sales cycle. And those same tools will help build your credibility and help the most likely prospects get ready to work with you.

Teaching for free or next to nothing

Some organizations, businesses and institutions may want offer to pay you to teach a free class for their members. You may initially look at this and see that you're receiving your consulting rate for a full hour. However, you're dispersing your knowledge for very little pay to a group of people who have not been charged anything and thus now see your information as "free". Make sure you build in the full costs of your time, along with the value of the information. If you're teaching a one-hour course for $150 and your consulting rate is $150, you're doing an awful lot of work for that rate. Most instructors will tell you that one hour of class time involves three hours of prep time – and sometimes more. If you've taught the class multiple times, you may achieve some efficiencies, so aim to build reusable content.

If you do decide to teach a class for a lower rate, be clear on what you're getting out of it. In some cases, the audience may be made up of prospective clients, giving you the chance to generate and capture leads. Or perhaps speaking at a prestigious organization is part of the marketing clout you're seeking to build. Whatever the case, be clear on your purpose and your returns. And remember that paid work trumps free work, when it comes to credibility and your cash flow. If doing more prestigious work for free fails to result in more work from a paying client, it obviously also fails on value.

Negotiating fees

Once you've set your consulting fees, you may run into clients who want to negotiate. There's no hard and fast rule for who'll want to negotiate. Some do, some don't. Recruiters seeking to place consultants often dangle high rates when they pitch the position, but later try to haggle with you.

Some consultants say never negotiate price. When you try to compete on price, you imply that your work is a commodity and that the rates you set are unrelated to your true value. You suggest that everything is negotiable, perhaps setting a bad precedent for the rest of the project.

Still, sometimes, it makes sense to negotiate. You're still at the stage where you're trying to understand the expectations of all involved. You may have misinterpreted the client's needs, meaning you've allowed more time for certain project tasks than necessary. You may have assumed a certain level of handholding, when the client is actually very independent. So, if a client asks you to drop your price, instead find out if you have met their expectations. Have a discussion with them. Explore one another's needs and positions. Negotiate the project terms, not the fee you quoted for the original proposal.

For example, let's say you quoted on rewriting a client's business plan. You may have assumed that the client wants to review, edit and make comments on paper copies, which they will mail, fax or courier back to you. However, perhaps the client would be open to making those changes in a word-processing program and emailing the document to you, so that you can more quickly review and accept their changes.

Or consider a situation in which you quoted on carrying out research at the library. After talking to the client, you find out that they already have reams of data to share and that they also have an online subscription to journal databases. This dramatically cuts time spent at the library, leaving you with room to adjust your quote.

Those are all reasons to consider negotiating a project. However, sometimes you'll run into a client who really wants to negotiate a price. Some people have been told that consultants expect people to negotiate rates. Others come from cultures, countries or industries where haggling is a welcome part of the business process. You may even share this belief. So, if you want to negotiate, feel free. Know what your goals are and what you're willing to compromise on. Look for mutual ground. But negotiate strategically! When you negotiate fees, you have several starting options:

- **Bid as though money is no object.** This is pretty confident, but you'll probably scare away your client. Respect your client's budget and need to turn a profit. Besides, if you've gone through the process of setting your consulting fees, you should strive to provide realistic quotes. And, if you're in tune with the client's needs, you should be able to keep your proposal to just the consulting services that will meet their needs.

- **Start with your walk-away price.** This may make you look attractive to price-sensitive clients, but, if the client wants to negotiate, you have no where to go. You also suggest that you're hungry for work or that you don't know your own worth. And, since you've already indicated you're willing to negotiate by taking part in the exchange, it doesn't really make sense to start with a price that would cause you to end the discussion.

- **Bid at the low end of fair.** This is better than selling yourself short, but still isn't a great place to start. If your client wants to negotiate, you have little wiggle room. You could consider using this as a loss leader to entice a new client to try you out, but do keep in mind that you're setting the client's expectations.

- **Use the maximum for your range.** You're showing you value your time and that you think you're a serious contender. You're also giving the client room to negotiate. However, you may price yourself out of the market, if someone "almost as good" or "just as good" quotes just below you.

- **Quote five to 20 percent above what you want.** This shows you're confident in your own abilities, without making you look arrogant or unrealistic. It also allows you to negotiate your fees, without pushing yourself below fair market value.

- **Provide a flat, firm Solution-Based Fee price.** If you're ready for this stage in consulting, you will move the focus to the value your solution provides for the client, not the fee you charge. See Part II of this book for details.

Fig. 7: Summary of options for negotiating fees:

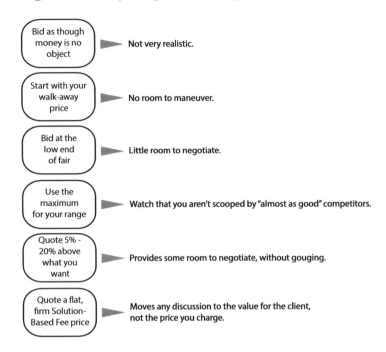

Bid as though money is no object	Not very realistic.
Start with your walk-away price	No room to maneuver.
Bid at the low end of fair	Little room to negotiate.
Use the maximum for your range	Watch that you aren't scooped by "almost as good" competitors.
Quote 5% - 20% above what you want	Provides some room to negotiate, without gouging.
Quote a flat, firm Solution-Based Fee price	Moves any discussion to the value for the client, not the price you charge.

Still, unless you're from an industry or culture where everything gets negotiated, you should aim to make firm, transparent quotes to your clients and use clear, detailed proposals that set out the project deliverables, milestones and fees. That way, they know where you stand and you can focus on the work, not banging the fees and proposal around till you're both sure of things.

Consultant Profile:
Jennifer LaFrance, jaelynnconsulting@att.net

Q: Tell me about your business.

I am a training consultant; I facilitate workshops on sales, coaching and leadership courses I have been in business for 3 years.

Q: How did you get started?

I initially started because a training vendor wanted to hire me as an independent contractor to work with their clients.

Q: How did you come up with your fees?

I still struggle with fees; your ebook has been EXCELLENT in helping me feel more comfortable with my worth. I basically researched and determined the competitive rate on the market for my services

Q: How do you feel about money, revenue and pricing?

I am TOTALLY green and am still in the process of figuring all of this out.

Q: What advice would you give to other people thinking about their fees?

Think carefully about what you bring to the table; we often underestimate our worth and do not realize that education, life experiences and work experiences are very valuable to someone.

Notes, Thoughts and Questions about this Chapter

Things I want to consider:

Things that occurred to me:

Questions I have:

For anything worth having, one must pay the price; and the price is always work, patience, love, self-sacrifice — no paper currency, no promises to pay, but the gold of real service.

~ John Burroughs

CHAPTER 7

Avoiding Price Wars

As you go about making proposals to clients, you may run into some challenging situations. Some clients may try to haggle, while others may try to push the project scope. Others may try to make you feel guilty about your rates. Some may tell you that they always go with the lowest bid. Well, if you keep running into these situations, the problem isn't the client. It's how you feel about your own work.

You see, if you're completely confident in your own positioning, offering, work and fees, you won't feel like there's an onslaught of client management issues. You'll be able to brush off any pressure clients apply. You'll be in a position to contain your feelings, because you won't have uncertainty busting through.

Managing lowest bid situations

Sometimes clients will inform you that they are gathering several proposals or quotes and that they will be selecting the lowest bid. If you choose to compete in such a scheme, you effectively reduce your services to a commodity. You imply that your skills, services and solutions are no better than those of your competitors. Unless you have a desire to send this message, steer clear of lowest bid competitions.

Determining affordability

Many consultants get hung up on how much they think their clients can afford. They worry that they will out-price themselves and leave their clients unable to afford their work. If this is the way you think, you need to consider things from a different angle.

As a consultant, you solve problems for people. The solutions you develop save them time, energy and money. Instead of asking what your clients can afford to pay, think about what value you create for them. People don't buy things because they can afford them. They buy things because they want to solve a problem. If you focus on solving your client's problems, your fee becomes a minor point.

Handling objections to price

From time to time, clients will object to your quotes. If no one ever protests, you're probably charging too little. Remember, a certain number of customers will always think you're charging too much, no matter what your price. You should aim to meet the price expectations of about 80 percent of clients in your target market.

However, when people object to your fees, their concerns may be valid. You should listen to them with open ears and an open heart. Connect with their emotions. Listen to what they want from you. Position your services as a solution to their problems and as a way of fulfilling their goals. Emphasize the solution and services they'll receive from you. By reacting in this way – rather than haggling over price – you keep the focus on the client and the value of your services.

Figure 8: Consider your clients objectively

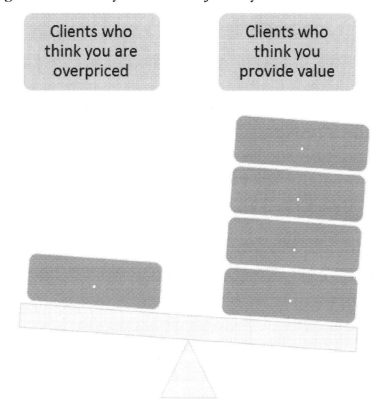

Raising your rates

Whether you've been trucking along as a consultant for years or you're brand-new at the game, you'll eventually need to raise your rates. After all, your skills and productivity will have improved and there's that little matter of the cost of living. In raising your rates, you may occasionally lose clients, but most people understand inflation and realize that you've got to keep up with costs.

However, some clients will actually see your price increase as a positive. Many people associate higher prices with higher quality, status and credibility.

When you raise your rates, you suggest you deliver high quality work. By charging higher rates, you test the price elasticity of the market. Clients know that, if you can charge more, you must be in demand. If you were starving for work, you wouldn't be able to charge such high prices – or so they think.

Some clients react to higher fees as if they were status symbols. For example, when I worked for a major utility company 15 years ago, one of my coworkers bragged that she had hired a technical writing consultant "who charges $125 an hour when everybody else charges $85, so you know that he's got to be the best". I never met the man, but I've always remembered his name – and today his consulting business has expanded to employ several people.

Clients also see higher fees as reassurance. For some, hiring a consultant is a risky proposition. They're opening their organization to an outsider, using a good portion of their budget to do so, and putting themselves out on a limb. These people often see your higher rates as an indication that others value your work. They infer that you wouldn't be able to charge those rates if other clients were balking. And, if something does go wrong, they can show their manager the quotes from other "top consultants" and show that you were one of the best in the market. For these clients, you provide reassurance when you raise rates.

Making more without hiking your fees

As a consultant, you can make money in one of five ways. You can raise your fees, work more hours, become more efficient, or cut your costs – or move to Solution-Based Fee pricing. Cutting costs can sometimes be the easiest solution, if you don't want to rock the boat, take on more work or change how you work.

Barter

Many consultants engage in barter. Although formal barter exchanges exist, most people do barter the old-fashioned way. My consultant friends have traded their consulting services for graphic design, marketing, accounting, Wordpress consulting, use of a ski resort condo, writing, childcare, administrative help, household help, cleaning services and more. Do note that most governments treat barter as taxable revenue, so you may need to declare this "income" on your taxes. However, you can also deduct the cost of "buying" the other party's services. Check with the IRS or your country's tax authorities for details.

Cooperative Marketing

To cut costs, many businesses take part in cooperative marketing and networking. By piggybacking on the marketing and networking endeavors of other consultants, they leverage great tools without incurring great expenses. Some ideas for cooperative marketing and networking include:

- Arranging for a profile on another consultant's website. (For example, realtors often promote their relationships with mortgage brokers, movers, contractors and cleaners.)

- Sharing ad space with another consultant. (In my hometown, bookstore owners often put together their own "independent bookstore" ad, splitting the space among several stores.)

- Co-writing an article for a trade publication

- Sharing sponsorship of an event

- Co-hosting a seminar, workshop, public lecture or webcast

- Promoting one another in client newsletters

- Providing referrals to one another

- Offering the colleague's marketing materials in tradeshow booths, offices, information kits or even a link on a blog or ebook

- Jointly issuing a press release

- Sharing administrative help

Rent, borrow and buy used

If cash is tight, consider leasing or renting equipment, rather than paying cash upfront or financing your purchase with a high interest credit card.

Let friends, family and colleagues know you're looking for a particular piece of equipment. You may find out that someone has a computer monitor, printer, desk or chair sitting in their garage. Many people would be happy to lend or sell their unused items.

Check your local online and newspaper classifieds for used equipment. Office furniture, printers, computers, supplies and other materials often show up at auctions, classifieds and office clearance centers.

Work from home

As many home-based consultants have learned, working from your basement, den or a corner of your home can deliver tremendous cost savings. By avoiding the costs associated with setting up an office, you free up cash for other activities. Moreover, depending on your jurisdiction, you may be able to write off your business use of home.

Maximizing billable hours

As a consultant, you can only work so many hours in a day. Administration, family, recreation, sleep and activities limit just how much you can work. So it makes sense to reduce time spent on administration and to look for other ways to boost productivity. (And, when you're ready, it makes sense to move to Solution-Based Fees — but more on that later.)

Assistants

Hire an assistant to help you with routine and tedious administrative work, such as filing, photocopying, opening mail, formatting documents or running errands. Although administrative assistants provide a valuable service, they usually bill less per hour than do consultants. So, if you replace time spent on administration with billable hours, you can earn more money. Say — isn't that what you tell your own clients?

Sales help

If you can't find time to market and sell your services, you'll soon find you don't have enough business. However, when business is great, it's often hard to force yourself to keep looking for new work. Consider hiring someone to help you with your sales and marketing. Even a neighborhood college student may be a great help in responding to inquiries, mailing out information packages, putting together a client newsletter, or coordinating a direct mail campaign.

Outsource

Like other small business owners, consultants often find themselves wearing many hats. So try to reduce the non-billable time you spend on work outside your core services. Look at outsourcing your accounting, sales, marketing, administration, office cleaning, computer repair, tech support, writing, editing and other projects. There are lots of other consultants who'd be pleased to do the work, so you can make more money doing what you do best.

Automate administration

Wherever possible, automate administration. Set up your bills to go to your credit card or bank account. Use invoicing and accounting software to manage your finances. Set up your email to filter incoming messages. Try to reduce the time you spend on routine non-billable work.

Ready for more? Then you may be ready to move on to Solution-Based Fee pricing....

Notes, Thoughts and Questions about this Chapter

Things I want to consider:

Things that occurred to me:

Questions I have:

SECTION II:
SOLUTION-BASED FEES

The purpose of business is to create and keep a customer.

~ Peter Drucker

CHAPTER 8

Moving to Solution-Based Fee™ Pricing

Small business owners often struggle with pricing things right. And with rising costs and a rapidly changing marketplace, figuring out what to charge can be daunting. But shifting to premium pricing requires a shift in mindset, starting with an understanding of the flaws in traditional pricing and moving to a model where value drives fees.

Under Solution-Based Fee pricing, you charge for the value of the solution you deliver to your client. Rather than simply looking at what it costs you to produce a solution or what your labour is worth, you create pricing based on the solution you offer.

Running a business takes hard work. And it can be darn frustrating to see yourself getting the short end of the stick. In a time when it seems like cutbacks are inevitable, it can be tempting to start slashing your prices. But, really, once you start cutting your prices, you're in a race to the bottom of the pool. First you cut your rates, then your competitors cut their rates… it's not long till you're all hoping for a few measly crumbs at the bottom.

Besides, the customers who chase prices won't be loyal. They'll go wherever they can find a deal. Some of them will do whatever it takes to get a deal, because they care more about the satisfaction of the hunt than they do about what they get served up with their deal. Or, if they do find the deal of the century, their loyalty will hinge on the price. Raise the prices and they'll be off in search of the next deal.

Maybe you have thought about raising your prices, but you're not sure how to do it. For a lot of people, money is one of those subjects you're not supposed to talk about. In fact, some people grow up in families or cultures where money is never discussed. And that's fine – everybody's different. But, if you're in business in mainstream North American in the early 21st century, you may need to take a different approach.

Take this, for example. Mary, a local graphic designer has amazing talent. She turns around calls quickly. She gets work done on time and for a great price. She gets rave reviews from clients. But, time and time again, she sees prospective clients choosing her competitors – who charge 50 percent more. She's left scratching her head, wondering what went wrong.

Well, Mary's competitors post their portfolio pieces online. Their website outlines how they work. When you call them, they listen, reflect back your concerns and ask you how things would change if your concerns were addressed. They follow up with a courteous email, a professionally formatted proposal, words that address your pains and build on your vision of a solution and include customer testimonials, a case study and a call. So, even though they charge more than Mary, they leave prospective customers feeling very comfortable that they are dealing with a qualified, professional firm that's worth the money.

But Mary could change this. She could take steps to put together a strategy and tools to support price increases. Because, at the end of the day, good clients – the ones who want more than a deal – make their decisions based on solutions. If Mary builds a case for the solution and value she provides and draws a map that shows customers how she can provide that value for them and build on their vision, she can win bigger and better deals and charge more.

The basis of Solution-Based Fee™ pricing

A price boils down to what you expect to be paid for your goods and services. From the customer's point of view, it's what they will have to pay you to get those same goods and services.

Traditionally, when we think about price, we consider the cost of producing the goods and services, features, the conditions of the market, competitors' positioning, market conditions and quality.

With solution-based pricing, we draw the customers' attention to the value they get from the complete solution. This means emphasizing features, benefits, quality and the vision that the solution will help them achieve. In working with the client to create a vision of how that solution will change their situation, we can shift the emphasis to the value the client gets from the solution, rather than the cost of providing consulting. No one really wants to buy consulting – but most clients are open to means of solving problems and delivering solild returns on their investments.

If you are used to looking at pricing from the point of view of costs, such as the inputs you use or your hourly rate, you will struggle to get top dollar for what you have to offer.

The problem with traditional cost- and time-based pricing

Time-based pricing

For example, let's say you become a plumber. When you start out, you charge just a little below what everyone else in the market charges. Your rate is $65 an hour. In general, once you account for breaks, you work about seven hours a day for a total of three customers, on average. Your total daily billing works out to $455 a day. You work 20 days a month for 11 months of the year, once you adjust for vacation, sick time and stat holidays. That means you bill about $100,100 a year – before you deduct the cost of tools, transportation, bookkeeping, phone costs and so on.

Over the years, you become an excellent plumber. You are much better at what you do now and you can complete jobs in half the time that it used to take you. In seven hours, you can now complete six jobs. And guess what? Unless you raise your rate, you will only make as much as you did before, only now you are doing far more work.

But let's say you double your rate to make up for how quickly you work. Well, there's just one problem with that. When potential customers call around to ask for rates, you will be quoting $130 an hour, while everyone else quotes $65, $75 or even $100. "But I work faster!" you say. That's a big leap of faith for the customer who pays by the hour.

Cost-plus pricing

You want to work 20 days a month, 11 months of the year, since you want some vacation, sick time and stat holidays. That's 220 working days a year. Given seven hours a day, that's 1540 hours you work each year.

You figure you have fixed costs to cover each year. Rent, utilities, Internet, phone, supplies, tools, equipment, transportation and so on. That works out to $20,000 a year. Worked out by the hour, that's $12.99 you need to cover for every hour you work.

If you were working at a job somewhere, you would earn $35 an hour, with benefits.

So you add your old hourly rate to your business costs. $12.99 + $35 = $47.99. You round off and come up with $48 an hour.

But you didn't go into business just to make what you made before. After all, you want to turn a profit. So you figure you should make 33 percent profit on your labour. That works out to $63.84, so you round it up to $65.

Now you are in the same position as the hourly rate example above. The only way to get ahead is to raise your hourly rate. And that just draws the customer's attention to costs.

Or let's say you have a product. It will revolutionize the world. In fact, it can save people time and money. It costs you $15 to manufacture and distribute. So you mark up the price to $30. You sell 5,000 products a year – and, in return, you earn revenues of $150,000 with profits of $75,000. The only way to make more is to sell more or to cut your price.

See the problem with using your time or your costs in working out your fees? Sure, it will work in a pinch, but it means that the more efficient or valuable you are, the less you see a return from your efforts.

Enter Solution-Based Fee pricing. With Solution-Based Fee pricing, you shift the customer's focus to the value your entire solution creates for them.

With Solution-Based Fee pricing, you shift the buyer's attention to the value you create for them. It's harder for a buyer to be price sensitive if they can clearly see that they will make more money or save more money by using your service. If they see your service as clearly valuable, they will stop using low-cost comparisons when they think about price. When they perceive your solution as higher quality and clearly in line with the solution they seek, they will more easily part with their hard-earned dollars.

Why selling doesn't work

Do you like to feel sold? Of course not. Nobody does. People like to buy. Think of all the excitement people have when they tell you about a great new product or service they found. People love to feel like they got something that really worked for them – a great solution that brings value to their lives. But nobody likes to feel like they've been sold.

When you feel like you've been sold on something, you might feel like you were pressured too much. Or that you got tricked into making a purchase. Maybe you didn't get what you thought you were buying. The thing is, though, nobody likes that feeling. People don't want to be sold – they want to buy. Yet most businesses focus on selling.

The probably with a sales focus is that you're pushing things on your clients. Instead, if you take a solution-based approach, you look at the challenges your clients have. You take time to get to know them and understand the implications those problems have for their businesses. Then, when you make a proposal, you highlight the implications of those problems and the consequences for the client. And then you're at the point where you can propose a solution and talk about the value it will create for your client.

Mentally preparing to ask for more

When we talk about shifting to solution-based pricing, you may first think this involves a huge effort in changing the mindset of your current and potential customers. But there's actually someone else who has a mind you need to change first.

You.

You see, preparing to charge more takes a certain attitude. A certain degree of confidence. If your own foundations are shaky, how will you stand up to the scrutiny of customers? Why pricing based on solution value delivers the best profits

It makes sense to price based on the value of your solution. If you shift the customer's attention to how long it takes you to do something, you're almost begging them to set the meter running in their mind. Their focus will be on how much it costs, not what it gets them. Likewise, if you price based on the cost of developing a solution, you put some serious limits on your earning potential.

Take yoga pants. How much can they really cost to manufacture? Well, if you're a little unscrupulous with your choice of manufacturer or the product quality, you can probably get them made for a few dollars. Let's say you double that. Well, uh, now you have a few more dollars. Not exactly a money maker, unless you have the capacity to sell hundreds of thousands of them.

But let's say you shift the buyer's attention to the challenge they have been having with their yoga class. The way the fabric pulls when they try to do lunges. Or how it rides up when they go into Child's Pose. Or perhaps the red marks that they get when the top rolls up. Or the way it wrinkles. Or leaves them wondering if they look good enough for yoga class.

Lululemon Athletica revolutionized the yoga clothing industry when it came on the scene in 1998. They got yoga instructors to wear the products and provide feedback. Of course, in doing so, they got influential people to wear their branded clothing, boosting the credibility of the products. And when lululemon opened its beach area store in trendy, yoga-loving Kitsilano in 2000, they created what they called a community hub for health living.[1] The company focused on training in-store educators to lead healthy lives and influence their families, communities and customers. What set Lululemon apart is that they realized their customers wanted more than just yoga wear. They wanted support in living a healthy lifestyle and they wanted that support from a credible source. In developing a portal for healthy living, lululemon met the whole needs of its customers.

Applying solution-based pricing to consulting

When you go into consulting, you go into the knowledge business. Does it really make sense to be charging by the hour? Well, in reality, you should be offering a solution to the client, not selling your time. If you come up with a fantastic solution in five minutes, you're not getting proper compensation and, honestly, the client won't care how long you took. They'll just be glad for the solution. With Solution-Based Fees, you create a solution for the client's problems and price accordingly.

There's an old joke[2] about physicist Niels Bohr that illustrates this principle. Bohr won the Nobel

---

1 "lululemon athletica: our company history". Retrieved 15 August 2011 from http://www.lululemon.com/about/history.

2 If you happen to know the original source for this joke, let me know. I've put it into my own words and spun it a bit for consulting, but it's based on a joke I had a few people tell me when I was still a student.

Prize, worked on the Manhattan Project and made major contributions to physics.

A company's machine breaks down. The company's owner, an old school chum of Niels Bohr, calls in the physicist for help in fixing it.

Bohr examines the machine. He draws an X on the side and says, "Hit it right here with a hammer."

The company's mechanic hits the machine with a hammer. It springs into action. The company's owner thanks Niels Bohr profusely and sends him on his way.

A few days later, the owner receives an invoice from Bohr for $10,000. Shocked, the owner phones Bohr!

"Niels! What's this $10,000? You were only here for 10 minutes! Send me a detailed invoice."

Bohr agrees to send the invoice. A few days later, the company's owner opens a new invoice.

INVOICE

Drawing X on the machine	$ 1
Knowing where to put the X	$ 9,999
Total	$ 10,000

As you can see, Solution-Based Fees are where you'll find the real money in consulting. After all, if you charge an hourly rate, you'll be constrained by the number of hours you could possibly work in a year. And, as you become more efficient, you'll have to keep raising your rates or you'll lose money. For example, if you can initially finish a job in four hours at $50 an hour but you later learn to do it in three, your earnings from the job would fall to $150, down from $200 when you were less efficient!

Solution-Based Fees draw attention to the value you provide when you solve a client's problem. For example, a number of years ago, I was working on pricing for a firm that had a new offering. This radical, new solution would almost eliminate the need for engineers to fly by helicopter into mountaintop locations in Southeast Asia. The solution was very inexpensive for to deliver, but it was going to save clients thousands of dollars. When you look at the value the solution provided, it would be ludicrous to stick to an hourly rate. So I recommended pricing at a level that was about 75 percent of the cost of flying in engineers. And I also recommended a marketing strategy that would position the solution as superior to flying in engineers, mainly because clients could be up and running faster, meaning they could reduce downtime and start bringing in money. If we'd gone with an hourly rate, we would have been selling the company short.

However, if you're just starting out in consulting or you don't have a way to guesstimate the value your solution provides, you may be more comfortable with using an hourly rate. By using this hourly rate to generously quote by the project, you can at least allow for some extra profit when you deliver projects ahead of schedule or through efficiencies.

Charging by the hour is a long term trap

Can you imagine a business where you could only make a fixed amount of product? You'd never be able to move far ahead – your destiny would be fixed.

Sure, you could raise prices, but perhaps demand would fall. Or maybe your competition would counter your price increases.

Well, many consultants fall into the long term trap of pricing their time by the hour. While this strategy may work for newer consultants who are still building businesses and testing the waters, it doesn't provide a lot of long term opportunity for growth. (But, if you're okay with your fees, don't feel pressured. Solution-based pricing is an option, not a command.)

As a consultant, just how many hours can you see working in a year? 40 hours a week, 48 weeks of the year? That's 1920 hours. At $50 an hour, the most you can make is $96,000. At $200, it's $384,000. But, really, can you see working that many billable hours in a year? You still need to market, service, and manage your business. Go back to the chapter where we looked at billable hours – most people are lucky to have 874 hours in a year. At $50 an hour, that's not quite $44,000 a year. At $200 an hour, it's just under $175,000. And, while making that much a year sounds attractive, you'll probably need to bring on help to help you sustain that hold in the market – and you may be frustrated by not being able to make anything beyond that, since there just aren't many more hours you can work. If you got into consulting for the lifestyle, you just may not want to be working such long hours.

Pricing by the hour – or by the day, which is really the same thing – leaves you boxed in.

The problem with hourly and per diem rates

If you become efficient at doing your work and you bill by the hour, you'll make less money. Worse yet, the more efficient you get at doing your work, the fewer hours you can bill for it!

Let's say you charge $50 per hour and it takes you 25.5 hours to complete a project. If you become more and more efficient at doing that work and you keep billing by the hour, you'll make less money. To keep up, you'll have to start raising your rate. If you find a way to do the job in 15 hours, you'll need to charge more than $82 per hour. But if your knowledge and experience allows you to do the job in half an hour, you'll have to charge $300 per hour. Just take a look at *Figure 9: Efficiency, Hourly Rates and Revenue.*

Figure 9: Efficiency, Hourly Rates and Revenue

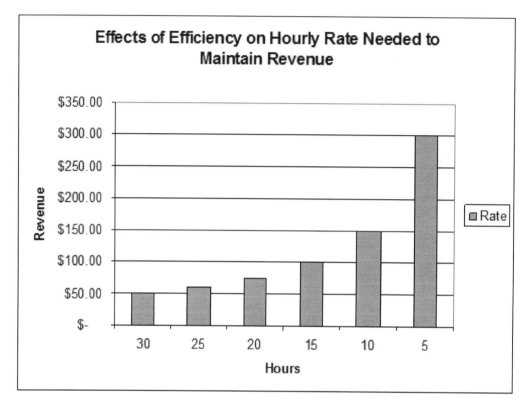

Yuck! Just because you've become great at doing your work, you're in a situation where you have to start cranking up your hourly rate, just to keep up with what you were earning before. Imagine you find a way to solve a problem in mere minutes – what do you do then? Charge $700 or more an hour? Lie and say it took you longer than it did?

If you prefer looking at it the other way, look what happens to your revenue if you don't raise rates. See *Figure 10: Effects of Efficiency on Revenue.*

Figure 10: Effects of Efficiency on Revenue

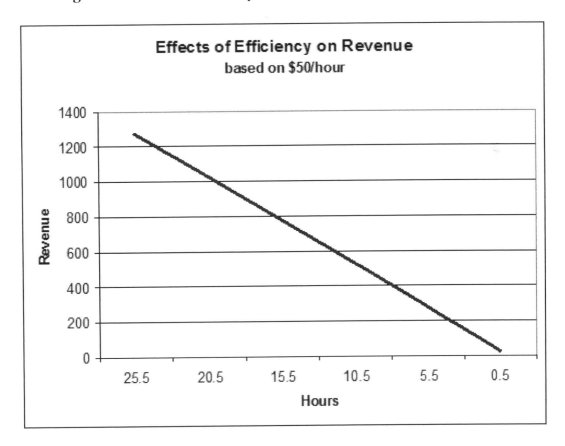

Now maybe you think that would never happen. But, when you're starting out, you're new to things. You may need to take more time to research solutions. You may be doing everything from scratch. After a few years, perhaps you will have standardized your tools and methodologies and maybe you can reuse information you uncovered for other clients. It's not unreasonable to think that you might sometimes have a solution instantly, whereas, sometime earlier, it would have taken you hours or even weeks. So why should you make less now that you're even more of an expert? And why should you have to distract the client with an hourly rate that may make them start thinking, "Hey, I don't make that! Why should YOU make that?"

Well, it's not just about the solution you offer. It's about the scarcity of that solution.

You see, producing a solution that saves your client thousands of dollars doesn't mean you should get a chunk of that savings. The real crux is how many other consultants could have done the same thing – in your client's eyes.

Your fees depend on whether your client believes your solution provides something that they won't get from other consultants.

The key then is to make your clients see your offering as scarce. It's not just about price – it's about ensuring that your client sees that you offer a compelling solution.

With billing by the project, the consultant (that's you) assumes the time risk. If you do the work faster than expected, you earn more than if you billed by the hour. Of course, if you underestimate the project, you end up making less per hour.

In comparison, the client takes on risk with billing by the hour. Many consultants prefer this set up because they feel safer from unknowns, such as fussy clients, delays and so on.

With billing by the hour, though, you run the risk of giving away your hard-won, high value knowledge for a pittance. Some consultants manage this by setting minimum rates – four-hours, per diem or even longer. But looking at your fees as part of your solution for the client can help you better build your business.

Fees are part of marketing

Your consulting fee is part of your marketing strategy.

Price is known as one of the four Ps of marketing – the others being product (and service), place and promotion. But, in setting consulting fees, many consultants overlook the connection between price and value.

Consider a scenario where three consulting firms are bidding on a job. Dana bids $25 per hour and estimates 100 hours. Joe bids $50 per hour, based on fifty hours. And Chris bids $3,500 for the project, setting out the outcomes to be achieved and offering a 30-minute debriefing and unlimited email follow up for 30 days after. All other things being equal, which consultant seems to offer the highest value?

From a dollars perspective, it looks like Dana will be $2,500, Joe will be $2,500 and Chris will be $3,500. But the numbers don't tell the whole story.

Dana seems to be priced low and to take a long time. Joe apparently commands a higher rate, which suggests more value, and does the work in half the time, which suggests better knowledge and improved productivity...or perhaps less attention to detail – it's hard to say. But Chris simply bids on the outcomes and will apparently be on hand to help with implementation and interpretation.

More importantly, Chris has taken the client's mind off the hourly rate and the amount of time involved in doing the work. Really, those are red herrings. What the client wants is a job done right – and to have a problem solved.

What's more is that Chris can actually do the job in 90 minutes. You see, Chris has come up with a methodology that speeds up projects like this one. Chris has invested hours in developing a solution that can be rolled out quickly – and that reflects the knowledge, experience and time Chris delivers. If Chris had to stick with an hourly rate, there would actually be a penalty for doing work quickly – unless Chris wanted to cite an hourly rate of $2,333. And, faced with telling a client that the hourly rate is more than a big city lawyer charges, well, who wants to do that? It makes far more sense to simply quote by the project.

Scarcity and demand

When you mark up your services with a profit, you're still pricing based on cost.

The real issue is the amount of trust between consultant and client. Clients want some sort of assurance that they're buying something real. That's why you can help manage the client's risk by providing strong branding, a consistent experience, testimonials, media coverage, articles and information products, third party endorsements and possibly even a guarantee.

But, you say, there are hundreds or thousands of consultants and consulting firms just like me! How can I make myself scarce?

Well, consider bottled water. You can get water just by turning on the tap. Still, you can go to the New York Ritz Hotel, where the water sommelier offers all you can drink for $5. Or you can buy Fernando Altamirano's luxury bottled water for $275, including shipping. You can also drive 45 minutes to your local warehouse club and pick up bottled water for about 30 cents a bottle. When you turn on a tap, you need to supply a clean container, cool the water and either clean up or dispose of the container. If you're in a restaurant, you may want a posh drink that complements the food. If you're into status symbols or art, maybe you want the stylish Altamirano bottle. If you want to be able to pull bottled water out of your fridge at home or the office, perhaps the warehouse water works for you. And, of course, there's also something to be said for taste. Even though water flows from your household tap, you may have a reason for choosing one of these solutions. Even if you decide to go with tap water, you'll find a range of companies offering everything from steel canteens to jugs with built-in filters.

Maybe you're worried that charging by the project will result in you eating your work. Well, sometimes it might. But if you've focused on doing your due diligence and standardizing your offering and aiming for efficiency that situation should be rare.

Make tough choices: use strategy

In looking at strategy, you have to start with Michael Porter. The world's best known business academic – a Harvard professor – took the strategy world by storm with his first book, in 1980. *Competitive Strategy: Techniques for Analyzing Industries and Competitors* (Free Press) is in its 53rd printing and has been translated into 17 languages.

Strategy is tough work. It means making hard decisions. That's because, if you have a strategy, it's ultimately different than that of anyone around you. You're on your own – you can't be all things to all people. In fact, if all the firms in a market offer the same thing, the only choice customers will have will be price. And pursuing price differentiation in an age where service work can be sent offshore is a sure fire race to the bottom.

Cost leadership

Under this Porter strategy, you gain market share by going after the most cost conscious customers. To do that, you need to have the lowest prices or at least the best value prices – or you need to offer your services at average prices while sustaining the lowest costs. If you want to make it with this strategy, you need the lowest costs. So you'll need to turnaround projects quickly, standardize your offering, offer no-frills, and limit customization or personalization. You'll want to keep your overhead low and have a cost conscious mindset. You may need to offer bulk pricing, work with low priced vendors, outsource overseas, squeeze your suppliers and so on.

But there's a problem with cost leadership. If your customer base thrives on low prices, you're sailing a sinking ship. If a competitor decides to undercut you, your customers will have loyalty to prices, not service. Moreover, if you decide you need to raise prices or if you want to shift to a different position later, you'll likely need to rebuild your market and rebrand your company.

Differentiation

Through differentiation, you create the perception of a unique offering, so that you can command a premium. Service, brand, features, reputation and other elements allow you to achieve this. Moreover, you build loyalty that overrides price sensitivity – and that same loyalty creates a barrier to entry for your competitors, since they will have to work hard to achieve what you've achieved.

Porter notes differentiation works when your target customers are not price sensitive, the market is competitive, customers have specific under-served needs, and your company has the ability to solve needs in a way that's difficult for competitors to copy.

Intellectual property, talented staff, innovative delivery and brand management can help you achieve this.

Focus

With focus, you determine the scope of your cost leadership or price differentiation. Porter says you can go for mass market appeal with a broad scope or a focused market segment with a narrow scope. If you pursue a focus strategy, you concentrate on a niche market. You need to excel at serving customers in that market, so that you build strong loyalty. But it's not enough to just focus on a niche market. You need to determine the scope of your market, then choose cost leadership or differentiation.

If you adapt a narrow focus, you develop a niche strategy for a few target markets. By focusing on one or two narrow markets, you can better meet the needs of your customers and develop innovative products and strong branding to reflect those needs. Ideally, you target customers who are less likely to seek out substitutes or those your competitors would be less capable of serving.

Figure 11: Porter's Generic Strategies at a Glance

		Competitive Advantage	
		Cost	Uniqueness
Scope	Narrow	Cost Leadership	Differentiation
	Broad	Focus (low-cost)	Focus (differentiation)

When you move to Solution-Based Fees, you work at delivering more than just your time. A true solution comes from more than just a service. It comes from the entire experience for the client – and it depends on how you package your services and differentiate yourself from other competing firms.

Notes, Thoughts and Questions about this Chapter

Things I want to consider:

Things that occurred to me:

Questions I have:

I think everybody's got a presentation. Everybody looks a certain way because they want to convey a certain image. You look a certain way because you want people to listen to you in a certain way.

~ Marilyn Manson

CHAPTER 9

Packaging Your Services

Imagine the paint is peeling off the windows in your living room. You've tried to figure out what's going on, but you can't get a paint store to give you a straight answer. A painter comes to your home and quotes an hourly rate. Let's say she's $75 per hour, plus paint and materials. She says it should take about four to eight hours, but there are many unknowns and she's not sure why the paint is peeling.

A second painter quotes $95 per hour, including paint and supplies, but also leaves the time estimate unknown. This painter says he can fix the peeling paint, but he hasn't quite figured out just what to do yet.

A third painter promises to fix the problem for $750, guaranteed. He provides reference letters and testimonials from 10 clients, including one that had peeling window frames. He's got professional looking materials, arrives on time, and assures you that he'll stick to the quote, no matter what. He emphasizes that he's pretty clear on how to fix the peeling paint problem, but that he'll guarantee his work and will come back if the windows start to peel in the next 18 months. He's been in business for 10 years.

Who would you choose?

While many of us understand the value of results-oriented pricing for other work, many consultants have not made the leap to Solution-Based Fees for the results they deliver. In fact, fantastic clients who instantly see solutions that save their clients big dollars often lose out by going with an hourly rate. At $200 per hour, you only get $200 for solving your client's problem in an hour. But at $50 an hour, if you take three days to solve the same problem, you get paid $1200!

Clients don't really care how much you charge per hour. They care about the problems their businesses have. They care about how those problems affect their profitability, which may include productivity, reputation or even just management headaches. If they're buying services for themselves, their concerns focus on their personal needs, such as safety, security, health, esteem and so on. Most clients will pay a premium if they believe a consultant will help them gain faster, better or longer lasting results. The key thing is that the client cares about what the results do for them or their business. They don't really care how much time or effort it takes you to solve the problem. They just want the problem to go away.

Of course, many clients are used to comparing hourly rates and time estimates. Some may think a higher rate suggests the consultant has more expertise. Some may get caught up in how much time the consultant is putting into the project. They may think the consultant is spending too much or too little time on the work – and they may attempt to negotiate that time.

By going with a Solution-Based Fee, you take away the client's temptation to dicker over your sticker price. They won't know your hourly rate or how much time is involved. Instead, you frame your proposal in terms of their problems, your ability to solve them, the value you bring, and the fee.

Supercharging your trusted status

Once you understand what it takes to charge more now, it's time to start building the relationships that will lead you to trusted status – and true profits. Supercharging your trusted status begins with building a real relationship with your clients and shifting your business to support them.

Trust comes from that gut feeling you get about whether someone will follow through. When you feel like you can really trust someone – or something or a company or a brand – you can relax. You can have confidence that they will perform a certain way – that they will meet your standards for quality in product and service.

Consider Starbucks for a moment. Starbucks is a well trusted brand. When you go into a Starbucks, you know that there will be light, relaxing music playing. There were be some clean, comfortable seats in good condition and that you can choose from a more private seat or a table where you can work at a laptop. You know that the sizes, drinks and items on offer are standard and that you can get something to eat there, too. In fact, you probably expect that there's a little deli bar of grab and go foods and a basket of chips and popcorn, as well as some chocolates and cookies at the counter. You'll be greeted by a smiling barista in a green apron. You know that they'll take your order quickly and that you just walk along to the end of the counter to get your drink, then move to the bar for a lid, sugar, cream, napkins and more. Should there be the slightest problem, you can easily get the attention of staff, who have the power to respond to your needs with a card for a free drink of your choice or escalate your concerns. While you're there, you can post on the community board, take advantage of the free Wi-Fi and work, chat, relax or head out the door. And that all comes down to trust.

You see, you may not like Starbucks. But you can trust it to do certain things, like provide a clean place to eat and drink. You can trust it to be predictable, so you can schedule a business meeting – or a date -- at a location you've never been to. You can dash into a Starbucks anywhere in the world and have a pretty good idea of what you're going to get. If you're a Starbucks fan, then you know you can trust any shop's beans to have that familiar flavour.

And trust – whether it's in a person, business or brand – really helps. Maurice E. Schweitzer, a professor at Wharton, notes:

Trust is like lubrication. It makes transactions easier, faster, cheaper. It fuels the economy, so we can trade. And we've lost some of that trust. So now the costs are going to go up. There's more friction, as we have to do more due diligence. I think that's necessary.

And clearly, it was necessary before this. So perhaps the silver lining is that we're going to get back to these basic principles of oversight and diversification[1].

Trust matters. People place a lot of value on trust. If they didn't, we wouldn't see the stock market tumble when a country or corporation fails to meet a goal. In fact, Edelmann, one of the biggest public relations companies in the world, takes an annual measure of trust. This study, called the Edelmann Trust Barometer, surveyed more than 5,000 high income earners in 2011[2]. In order of importance, people ranked the following factors for corporate reputation:

- High quality products or services

- Transparent and honest business practices

- Company I can trust

- Treats employees well

- Communicates frequently

- And people look for spokespersons with credentials, placing "experts" at the top for trusted sources3:

- An academic or expert

- Technical expert within the company

---

1 The Bernard Madoff Case: Trust Takes Another Blow. Knowledge @ Wharton. 7 January 2009. Accessed 25 March 2009 at http://knowledge.wharton.upenn.edu/article.cfm?articleid=2131.

2 Edelmann Trust Barometer Presentation. Accessed 22 August 2011 at http://www.edelman.com/trust/2011/.

3 Edelmann Trust Barometer Presentation. Accessed 22 August 2011 at http://www.edelman.com/trust/2011/.

- A financial or industry analyst

- CEO

- Non-government organization representative

People need to hear things repeatedly to believe them[4]. Edelmann found about 59% of people said they have to hear something three to five times before they believe it. But when they distrust a company, 57 percent will believe negative information after 1-2 times. When they trust a company, 51 percent will believe positive information after 1-2 times. Trust – and the lack of it – goes a long way toward influencing how people think.

When you have the trust of people in your market, your business can run more efficiently and affordably. That's because you will need to go to less trouble to convince them of the good your company does. Trust can give your business that little something that helps it stand out from the pack.

Differentiate using trust

In business speak, we call building trust differentiation for competitive advantage. And that edge over the competition can have huge effects. Customers will be less likely to shop around. They will spend less time questioning your business and your processes. They will get ready to buy faster. And they will be less likely to pay attention to what your competitors are doing.

---

4 Edelmann Trust Barometer Presentation. Accessed 22 August 2011 at http://www.edelman.com/trust/2011/.

Repositioning for Solution-Based Fee™ pricing

To go target clients who trust and value your solutions, you may need to make some changes. This may mean repacking your marketing materials – or even making changes to the way you look, talk or network.

Target visionaries

Wherever possible, go after executive decision-makers who see themselves as visionaries. These people easily envision the results your services can deliver. As a result, they are less price sensitive – they don't dicker over dollars when they're out to save or make millions.

Provide services others don't

To keep people focused on the value of your consulting services, bundle more value into consulting. Provide services other consultants don't. For example, one fitness consultant I know revamped her practice to target pregnant mothers and new moms. Whereas there are thousands of fitness consultants in her region, she's just one of a handful of prenatal and postnatal fitness providers.

Make your work look specialized

Price sensitive clients often look for ways to reduce their reliance on your services. So, counter by making it look impossible for the client to do your work in-house. Focus on using your specialized skills, experience and contacts. Remind clients of your special knowledge by occasionally sharing articles, referrals, successes and industry news.

Look like a duck, quack like a duck

Present yourself as if you are at the same level as your clients – even if they're richer and more successful. Now, if you're in a traditional consulting role, it makes sense to invest in a quality tailored suit, briefcase and other accessories. But if you're doing a different kind of consulting – such as fitness consulting, home renovations or even wilderness adventure tourism leadership – you may have a different "uniform". Whatever the norm for your business, be sure to present yourself professionally and within the expectation range of your clients. Hand out professionally designed business cards. And, when people ask you, "How's business?" answer honestly, but positively.

Know their world

To blend in with solution-oriented clients, you need to seem like you're one of them. Whether it's golf, cars, vacations, restaurants, books, theatre or parenting, keep on top of your target clients' interests. You don't actually have to take up these activities – just stay abreast of the latest news and trends. But be genuine – people can spot a fraud from a mile away.

Meet like-minded people

If you want to go after solution-oriented clients who will value what you offer, go to places where you're likely to meet them or be referred to them. Attend networking events where you're likely to meet clients from the same industry or background. Be genuine in your interactions and look to build relationships with people you can actually help. In time, you'll have a solid network of people with whom you can do business.

Building your company into a solution-oriented firm

Moving to Solution-Based Fees means building your company into a solution-oriented firm. Your marketing, sales and services need to align with the problems your clients face – and convince clients that you're the right firm to solve those problems.

Can you show you deliver measurable results?

Show the return on investment. Show how your fees and results offset the cost of your services. Emphasize your proven history of delivering that ROI. To do this, you'll need a set of client references, case studies, success stories, third party endorsements and testimonials. Getting articles published online or in print can also go a long way to building your reputation.

Is the client actually willing and able to implement your recommendations so that results can be achieved?

Sometimes clients just want a sounding board or an outside opinion – they don't actually want to follow through.

Can you stomach the best and worst case situations? How will change affect your business?

Are your clients willing to change? If not, are you willing to change clients?

Do you have a strong brand?

When I say "brand", I'm not just asking about your logo or your tagline. Does everything your customer touches – from your website to your brochures to your reports to your emails – work together? Are your discussions and proposals in alignment? Do you have references from existing clients who help to build your brand? If you speak to your market with credibility and focus, clients will pay a premium to tap into that experience. So communicate your results clearly. Use case studies, testimonials, success stories, media coverage and your own storytelling to make your value clear.

Do you have a marketing system to support your business and clients?

In moving to Solution-Based Fees, you need to have all your marketing working as an integrated system. To keep the client's experience consistent, you'll need to think about the flow of "touches", from the first time they think of looking for help with their problem right through to them paying your invoice and referring you to their friends and colleagues.

Checklist for Solution-Based Fees

Are you ready for Solution-Based Fees?

- Business plan

- Marketing plan

- Solid understanding of your market

- Marketing system and marketing tools – your case studies, testimonials, references, website, proposals, newsletters and so on all work together as part of a strategic plan and cohesive messaging. You've got a full system built out to help you transition contacts along the pipeline.

- Strong brand

- Confidence and courage

- Sales skills – ability to find a fit, ask for the sale and close the deal

- Contract

- Efficient solution

By turning your services into packaged solutions, you can move ahead. With this approach, you charge a set price for a specific offering. You focus on becoming efficient at marketing, selling, delivering and servicing this solution.

Once you've packaged and standardized your offering, you can turn this package – complete with marketing and delivery – into set intellectual property. From there, you can hire, license or franchise your offering, often at a premium price.

Moving from hourly rates to Solution-Based Fees™

Making the change from an hourly rate to a solution-based fee takes some planning. If you've already taught your client to expect an hourly rate, you'll need to plan carefully. That's because you've already set your client's expectations. But you can manage those expectations and transform the way you do business.

When I moved to Solution-Based Fees, I simply put forward a proposal using a fixed fee per project. No one balked. So try going with that method, if it feels comfortable for you.

If you're uncertain about doing that, you could just try the following. Send your proposal, just like "normal". Outline the client's needs and your plans for meeting them. Indicate what they'll receive and what value this offers. (You don't have to name numbers – it could be that you're simply going to present them with a five-page report outlining _____.)

Then state your fee.

Set out the objectives for the current project, so that you avoid scope creep — and make sure that you set fees high enough to cover demanding clients.

If your client asks why you've moved to this fee arrangement, keep the focus on their needs. "With the way we were working before, it might have felt like there was a meter running. It might even have created some uncertainty, since the end fee was an unknown, and you might have been wondering whether each conversation was going to up the bill. The fee was a constant undercurrent. Since the focus should be on meeting your needs, I'd rather avoiding asking you to make a financial decision every time something comes up on this project. And I'm sure you'd rather that I have an incentive to get things done for you quickly and that I don't ever hesitate to help because of some sort of concern about how much work I've already put in. This way, we can keep the focus on a relationship that best solves your problems and meets the demands of your business. And we'll both have certainty about expectations for the project."

If they ask what's in it for you, be honest. Tell them that it helps if everyone knows everything up front. No one has to worry about the meter running and there's no need to keep making decisions about time as you go along. Everything included under the project scope is included.

Are you ready for solution-based fears? If you're unsure, maybe you need to work through your fears....

Consultant Profile:
Marketing for Free Agents
Harold Jarche
Jarche Consulting
www.jarche.com

As a free-agent there are great opportunities to integrate work and learning and that is by thinking of marketing as education, both for you and your clients. Since a one-person business doesn't have separate marketing and training departments, there's no need to worry about any turf wars. Marketing is the same as Learning & Development.

Marketing and education have certain similarities – gaining attention; getting your message across; and changing behaviour. Much of our learning is through conversations with others, as is marketing, or as the Cluetrain Manifesto states in Thesis #1 – Markets are conversation.

Without conversation (oral, written, graphical, physical) there are no social transactions. This has been the key aspect of the un-marketing approach for my own consulting business. Learning and working are mostly conversation as well. To market yourself as a free-agent online, start by giving. That means be a valued contributor to conversations with your professional community. Helping to educate potential clients is an excellent path to develop relationships

After several years of blogging and engaging in educational (un-marketing) conversations online, here are some of the tangible benefits to my business.

Many of these practices are interwoven with my personal knowledge management processes as well.

Using a feed reader (via RSS), saves a lot of time and bookmarking.

The information I get from blogs and Twitter is usually weeks ahead of the mainstream press. This is competitive intelligence.

By blogging and tweeting I have raised my profile on the web, which is cheap, but time-consuming, marketing.

I use my knowledge base of blogs posts when preparing reports, proposals and presentations. WordPress is an excellent tool and has become much easier to use with version 3.0.

Blogging forces me to think and reflect in order to write, so that what was just an idea in my mind becomes more concrete. I am better prepared when asked questions by potential clients.

Through blogging and Twitter I have met a number of business partners.

Online writing keeps me in touch with a lot of interesting people and expands my view of the world, providing new ideas for my business.

When I have a problem, especially a technical one, I post it on Twitter and usually get an informed answer within 24 hours. It's like a large performance support system.

My web presence allows people to get to know my opinions before they engage me as a consultant; saving time and potential frustrations.

Read Harold's entire post at http://www.jarche. com/2010/08/marketing-for-free-agents-redux/.

Notes, Thoughts and Questions about this Chapter

Things I want to consider:

Things that occurred to me:

Questions I have:

Whatever you fear most has no power…it is your fear that has the power.

~ Oprah Winfrey

CHAPTER 10

Uncovering Your Fears

Are you scared to ask for more? Are you scared to hold your ground? Does the mere discussion of money freak you out?

Let's say you've set your consulting fee at $2500. After meeting a new client and making a proposal, you have a good feeling. You confidently tell the client your rate. And the client comes back and says, "You seem like a great fit. I'd love to bring you on board. But I can only afford $1750." So you cut your rate, because the client seems like a great fit and it's really only your time, right?

But is that really true? You've just started a relationship with someone who has clearly indicated they believe in your value. You've put your services on sale at a deep discount (30 percent!) – and it wasn't even your decision. You've shifted power to the client, indicated that your value isn't solid, and you haven't even started working for them yet. How do you think that relationship is going to work out?

What if you had the power to stand up for yourself? Imagine if you instead said, "You said you wanted a consultant who could help you achieve your goal of

_____, so that you could solve this _____ problem. To do that, it's $2500."

Now, if the client still balks, you can offer other options. You could suggest other projects that might meet part of their goal – but you need to emphasize that your expert advice is that they pursue the $2500 project. Tell them that they know their business best and that they're in the best position to make a decision about what trade offs they want to make – but, that if they want to meet these goals and solve these problems, it costs $2500.

A few months ago, a client asked me for a proposal. I quoted about $25,000. The client came back and asked if I could come down 10 percent. "After all," he said, "It's only 10 percent. Everybody can move 10 percent, surely – and it's such a great opportunity for you to get on board with our firm." I admired his desire to get the best value for his money – and to put his business in the best possible position for success. And I told him that. And then I explained that the fee was $25,000, because I wanted to be able to do the best possible job for him and that it wouldn't be up to my standards to cut corners. I noted that he'd said he needed to solve these important problems so that he could take his product to market, with the goal of bringing in almost 10 times as much in investment capital in the next few months. I said that doing that would cost $25,000. And, to fit with his clever use of humor – he was a real jokester – I added a little quip about how I'd love to know where he kept finding businesses able to move 10 percent, since I'd asked my bank if I could hold back 10 percent of my mortgage payments but they kept saying something about not having room to do that. I wouldn't have added that for most clients, but this guy loved making jokes and I knew it would make him smile. And it did. More importantly, he agreed with me and paid me the $25,000, then hired me to do even more work. He also noted that he respected me for sticking to my rate.

Consultant Profile:

M.B.
Nour Services

Nour Services provides the assistance that you need so that management tasks become business functions - not chores. To perform these functions and keep your organization running in a cost-effective, time-efficient way, get to know Nour: choose to partner with the right skills and experience. Nour provides value to its clients and only takes on projects that helps improve lives. No less.

The engagements of Nour Services cover the operational functions of organizations: Financial management, Business planning, Human capital development, Marketing and communications, Research entry and analysis; policy recommendations, Seminars and workshops, Training and educational course development and delivery, and Organizational efficiencies and process development.

Q: How did you come up with your fees?

I wanted to earn the same hourly rate that matches my most recent salary and compared it to my market rates.

Q: How do you feel about money, revenue and pricing?

I hate having to put a dollar sign on my expertise, and having to convince people of the value that they're getting.

Q: What advice would you give to other people thinking about their fees?

Be strong about affirming the value of your services.

Naming your core fears

For many people, if they're asked to cut their rates, they simply do it. If you're one of these people, you need to think about what's getting between you and your ability to stand your ground and value yourself. For most people, it's fear. Perhaps you're afraid that you'll:

- End up in confrontation

- Be told you're not worth the money

- Upset the client

- Lose the job or the client

- Look like you're obsessed with money

- Become one of those "bad" people who does things for money

- Have to think about numbers...and you hate numbers

- Upset your partner because you turned down work

- Need to tell your kids that they won't be getting new iPods

- Miss out on the vacation you wanted

- Wind up flat broke, without a cent to your name

If fear is holding you back from asking for your rate, your problem is NOT with your fees. Your problem is that you need to work through deeper issues. And that's okay. Most of us have baggage of some sort. We all have things to work through. But you need to know that you can work through those issues – and you don't have to settle for working for peanuts.

When you think about setting your fees, what do you fear personally? What do you fear for your business?

Fears I have:

You have courage within you. You have the ability to get through this. Consider all the people in the world who find themselves faced with war, violence, abuse, poverty, disease and more. If you can find one percent of that courage, you can succeed. You simply need to figure out what's holding you back and come up with a plan for succeeding.

Now make no mistake: courage won't turn every business into a success. But sometimes courage means recognizing that you're in the wrong business. It means having the strength to make big changes. It may mean realizing that you're got your service offering all wrong. Or coming to the conclusion that you need to make a radical change to your skill set.

But you've got courage within you. You simply need to confront what's holding you back, so that your fears no longer control you. You don't want your fears to haunt you. As a business owner, you have the opportunity to solve problems.

Go back and look at your fears again.

Consultant Profile:

Chris Garrett, Consultant & Author

Chris consults, trains and speaks about internet marketing, blogging and new media. He has written five print books and many ebooks, including *ProBlogger: Secrets for Blogging Your Way to a Six-Figure Income.*

I see people get offered their "chance of a lifetime" and not take it, only to live with the regret. It seems the sting of regret about something you did not do is worse than regretting something you tried. Our "what if" fears tend to be overblown, and can cause us to not take risks that could be the trigger for wonderful outcomes.

Notes, Thoughts and Questions about this Chapter

Things I want to consider:

Things that occurred to me:

Questions I have:

Ordinary riches can be stolen; real riches cannot. In your soul are infinitely precious things that cannot be taken from you.

~ Oscar Wilde, The Soul of Man under Socialism, 1891

CHAPTER 11

Addressing Your Fears

Dealing With the Fear of Confrontation

Many people avoid conflict and confrontation. Usually, there's a negative self belief holding them back – a worry that they're not good enough or that their concerns and needs are less important than those of the other person, perhaps. But if you spend time avoiding conflict and confrontation, it means you're sacrificing your own needs, values and concerns. And how does that affect you? Perhaps it eats away at your feelings of self worth. Or it turns into resentment.

You can work through your fears. Try the following:

- Identify and address your core fear(s)

- Role play

- Get a mentor

- Journal – note your thinking patterns

- Generate plans for worst case scenarios

- Find out the other person's point of view. Dale Carnegie said, "Seek to understand, then to be understood." By taking the time to find out what the other person is saying, you remove the race to have your own point of view understood first. And you might be surprised by the other person's views – enough that you change your opinion or reaction.

- Broaden your view of the choices. Do you see conflict as an "us" or "them" situation, a situation where you end up winning or losing?

Really, there are at least five ways for any conflict to turn out, if not more:

- Reach a stalemate, with neither of you changing your point of view

- Take the view of the other person

- Have the other person take your point of view

- Walk away from one another

- Collaborate with the other person, giving respect to one another's beliefs, needs, choices and values.

If you choose to view the "conflict" as an opportunity for collaboration and discussion, you may be surprised by how your feelings change. You can still maintain your boundaries and values. If you find that the client has not respect for those, though, it's an early signal to find another client. Collaboration and discussion need not wind up in an unhappy commitment for you. You have choice.

Being told you're not worth it

If you're worried that you might be told you're not worth the fees you charge, you need to address the reasons for this fear. Is it that:

- Your brand doesn't match your fees?

- Your service level?

- You don't believe in what you offer?

- You're mismatched to the market?

- You think your opinion is less important?

- A central self esteem issue that goes beyond your business and perhaps has bothered you for a while?

- Something else?

Identify the core of your fear. What have you got to lose by being told you're not worth it? Focus on that concern and come up with a plan for addressing it. Perhaps you need to ramp up your marketing, collect more client testimonials, improve your customer service, focus on your core competencies or reposition your offering. Or maybe you need to address your self esteem and self confidence or even work through past upsets in your life.

Your life experiences have shaped who you are and they may even be affecting how you set your fees. If that's true for you, you're not alone. Tons of people find that past personal upsets and trauma affect their business lives. That's perfectly normal and understandable – but it doesn't have to be that way. You can do something about it, if you are ready to do the work – on your own, or perhaps with the help of a coach or counselor, depending on just what your circumstances are. You don't need a "big" reason to ask for help.

Upsetting the client

Think through the client's reaction. How do you think they'll react to your fee? Identify all the possible reactions and then come up with a script for dealing with each. You can practice responding in a mirror. You can also go back and look at the tips for dealing with confrontation, because an upset client is really the outcome of a confrontation, in some ways.

Losing the job or client

When you're running your own business, it's understandable that you might worry about losing work. The income may be what's paying your bills. The client may represent a strong reference or improve your firm's prestige and reputation. Maybe this client is a friend or other value contact. Perhaps you need this project to show the kinds of results you can deliver. Or maybe this is the only client you have – or practically the only client. Some ways you can work through this include:

- Build an emergency fund

- Diversify your client base

- Look to create multiple streams of income

- Get out of debt, so you're freer in your decisions

- Work on cash flow management, so that you can handle income fluctuations

- Gather testimonials, references, case studies and success stories from a variety of clients and projects

- Decide if perhaps you really just need to do this one time, while you work toward creating stability via the above tactics.

Being money-obsessed and bad

Are you concerned that talking money means you're a bad person? Maybe you worry that you're look money obsessed and that talking fees distracts from the project at hand. What is it that concerns you?

Maybe you think that talking money makes you a bad person. Is that really true, though? Does asking for a fee that values your business's contribution make you a bad person?

Depending on your cultural background and beliefs, you may be uncomfortable talking money. You may consider it to be an intensely private subject.

Hating numbers

If you have math anxiety, you're not alone. Many people feel stress when they encounter any sort of math. But math anxiety doesn't have to keep you from ever crunching numbers.

Consider actors, singers and other performers. Many of them have stage fright – yet going on the stage is the core of what they do! These people have learned to work through their fear – they may even still have that fear – and they still excel at their work. Stevie Nicks, Faith Hill, Andrea Bocelli and some of the most performers in the world struggle with stage fright:

A little bit of stage fright, then I'm ready.

~ Faith Hill

I have big, big stage fright.

~ Andrea Bocelli

If you have stage fright, it never goes away. But then I wonder: is the key to that magical performance because of the fear?

~ Stevie Nicks

You can work through math anxiety. Some steps other successful consultants have taken include:

- Never talking numbers on the fly. Say that you're think it over and get back to the client. Even if you like numbers, this is a great opportunity to think the situation through and position yourself to make a well considered proposal.

- Use spreadsheets. Putting all the information in front of you and then using spreadsheets to crunch it for you may give you more of a sense of control.

- Take a business math course.

- Standardize your fees so that you never have to vary your price.

- Come up with a list of potential client objections to fees and write out your responses. Memorize them.

- Work with an accountant.

- Enlist a bookkeeper.

- Reach out to others in your business circle. Feeling the support of others can help you build confidence.

If math anxiety plagues you, you might want to take a look at *Fear of Math: How to Get Over It and Get on With Your Life!* by Claudia Zaslavsky.

Upsetting your partner

If you have a partner, they're important. Their needs, goals, feelings and opinions matter. But if losing a single consulting gig is going to upset your partner, there's something more at work. You and your partner need to sit down and talk about your business and how it affects your lives together. Ideally, you have had this sort of discussion before and you have worked out some ways to address your individual and mutual hopes and concerns. Because, really, if the prospect of a single consulting job is causing huge conflict for your relationship, there's more to it. And taking the time to find out what that is will help you move to a better place in your life and relationship.

Upsetting your kids

Maybe you really want this job because it affects the quality of life you've laid out for your kids. That's understandable – I don't like disappointing my kids either. It's hard on kids (and their parents – heck, anyone, really!) when their household income goes through feast or famine cycles. But there are ways to manage those fluctuations. By working out a household budget based on reasonable income figures and setting aside an emergency fund, you can stabilize finances. Now, if you're in a position where your standard of living is in a serious state, you might want to think about how you could increase your revenues. But if one consulting gig is going to make or break your family's lifestyle, it may be time to sit down and look at what expectations are reasonable. Making changes in your business may mean some short term sacrifices, but with the aim of increasing revenues (or at least reducing your workload) over the long haul. Maybe you need to say "yes" to a few more jobs at your usual rate before you move on to solution-based pricing. It doesn't have to be all or nothing. Whatever the case, take some time to review your concerns and communicate with your family. Listen to them and work on solutions together, rather than bearing all your fears on your own shoulders.

Missing out on vacations and other dreams

Maybe you're worried that changing your pricing will mean you'll lose work. Perhaps you're concerned that, if you lose this one particular job, you won't be able to go on vacation this year – or meet some other goal. Well, maybe. But if you remain committed to solution-based pricing and follow through, you may find that you can work less or earn more – meaning you'll have more vacation and other rewards in the years ahead.

Winding up flat broke

Yikes! Who wants to be totally broke? If you're in a situation where each consulting project will totally make or break your financial situation, you may want to review your emergency plan, get a part-time job, go back to full-time work and consult part-time, cut back your spending or something else. But it's not the solution-based pricing that's putting you in this scenario. It's the structure of your overall finances and the fears you have about running a business. If you can address why you fear being flat broke – heck, maybe it's a reasonable consideration for you – you may need to look at how you're structuring your business. But going from an hourly rate to solution-based pricing is most likely not the real problem. In fact, solution-based pricing may give you the opportunity to earn more from every job and free up time in your week for more work – whether that's in your business or at another job.

And, really, whether you have a job or a business, you face some financial insecurity. It's about what you see as risk.

Someone with a supposedly secure day job could wake up one day to find out:

- Their boss has been fired and the new manager has it in for them
- Their company is downsizing
- Their company has been acquired and their job is on the line
- A young, fresh-faced kid has been hired into a position below them...and may be after their job
- Their industry is in a slump and the company may need to cut back on salaries
- The company owner is tired and is folding up the business

When you're an employee, you come up with plans for dealing with situations like those, so, as a business owner, you can do the same thing.

Wanting to give back

Maybe you resist charging a good rate because you're worried about the people who have to pay the bills.

You're concerned that it's a non-profit or a small business or maybe even a person who's scraping by.

Give because you can. Give because you are pure of heart. A real gift has nothing attached to it – no strings. A real gift comes from your awareness that it is a gift. It comes without burden for you or the recipient. In other words, you cannot be led to give. You have to get there yourself. You need to make a conscious decision and it has to be right – for you, for the recipient and for the demands on your time, budget and energy.

Plan and watch fear melt

Once you identify your fears and take a good look at the goals you want, your fear will start to melt away. Knowing what's holding you back and then taking steps to move forward – that's powerful, more powerful than your fears.

We are taught to understand, correctly, that courage is not the absence of fear, but the capacity for action despite our fears.

~ John McCain

Now, regardless of your political leanings, John McCain's words carry truth. Taking action can help melt away your fears and move you toward the business – and life – you want.

Notes, Thoughts and Questions about this Chapter

Things I want to consider:

Things that occurred to me:

Questions I have:

We must have a theme, a goal, a purpose in our lives. If you don't know where you're aiming, you don't have a goal. My goal is to live my life in such a way that when I die, someone can say, she cared.

~ Mary Kay Ash

CHAPTER 12

Realizing Your Fees Are Not Your Value

Remember, your consulting fees reflect the value of your solution – not your personal value. Your fees reflect the client's perception of the value of your solution, perceived risk, market rates, urgency, supply, demand and ease of substitution.

Go back and read that sentence again. You won't see a single word about your value as a person. Self worth refers to your ability to see yourself as successful and capable. The way you were treated by your family, peers and community, along with major life events and even traumas can shape your self worth. Learning to accept yourself – your strengths and your weaknesses – goes a long way toward creating high self worth. If you hold on to negative beliefs about yourself, you'll have lower self worth.

Self worth is important.

Some years ago, Abraham Maslow came up with a pyramid to show the various levels of human needs. *Figure 12: Maslow's Hierarchy of Needs* includes self esteem – or self worth. But here's something interesting – if your self esteem affects the way you do your work and charge and collect fees, it ends up affecting your basic safety needs! It's no wonder then that so many people get tired up in knots when they start thinking about their fees.

Figure 12: Maslow's Hierarchy of Needs

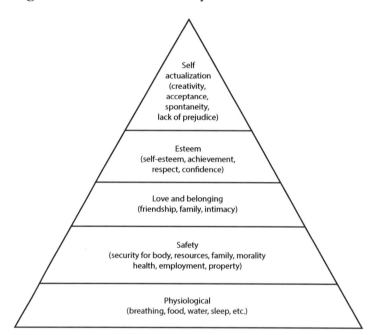

But, while your self worth may end up affecting your work, avoid temptation to equate your self worth with net worth. Your self worth refers to how you value yourself. Net worth simply boils down to assets minus liabilities. Whether you have all the money in the world or nary a cent, your value as a person can never be determined by a bank account – or by the fees you charge.

However, it's pretty common for people to knock down their fees because of problems with their self worth. A lot of people charge low fees because they struggle with how they perceive themselves. Try to think of yourself as a business so that you have some distance. If it helps, you might even rename your business to help achieve that personal distance.

Build self worth

If you want to try building your self worth:

- Pay it forward. Give love, hope, encouragement, opportunity.

- Live with courage and seek out opportunities that match your needs, goals and values.

- Embrace your weaknesses and, when you're ready, work on them or around them.

- Spend time with people who love you, care about you and treat you well

- Set attainable goals and work to reach them

- Ask for help

- Celebrate your accomplishments

- Hold fast to your values and integrity

- Take responsibility for yourself, your choices, your actions and your feelings

Notes, Thoughts and Questions about this Chapter

Things I want to consider:

Things that occurred to me:

Questions I have:

If you think nobody cares if you're alive, try missing a couple of car payments.

~ Attributed to Earl Wilson

CHAPTER 13

Getting Paid

No matter how high your fees or how busy your consulting schedule, you won't be successful if you don't get paid. Yet I meet many consultants who do business without contracts. Although verbal agreements are binding in many jurisdictions, it's a lot easier to use a written contract that outlines what you've promised the client and what the client has promised you.

When you use a contract, you come across as a professional, experienced businessperson. You also save yourself time and energy because, when issues arise, you can look to the contract as a guide in making decisions. Disputes over fees often come up when there is miscommunication over what work was to be done – and when and how.

Contracts can also help you encourage cash flow. By collecting deposits on work, billing after key milestones, and charging interest on overdue payments, you can ensure you have money coming in. One of the biggest reasons for business failure comes down to cash flow issues. If you don't collect your fees, it is certainly possible to go out of business despite working at full capacity.

Think that sounds ridiculous? Over the years, I have known many consultants who fell short on the invoicing side of things. Guilt, fear, shame, mathphobia, time management, computer skills and other issues sometimes complicate invoicing. In fact, once, I was called in to help a mid-sized company that was proud of its sales track record for the previous year. It turned out that they had not followed up on invoices for more than a year and had essentially shipped out seven-figures in product. Problems getting paid can happen to anyone, no matter how big or small your company may be. So get your work in writing and invoice promptly.

Tips for invoicing

Ask for a deposit. Invoice your client for the deposit when the project starts. It means you'll have cash on hand to get you through till the project's completion – and you'll be mitigating the risk of tying yourself up with the work.

- Tie your payments to key milestones. Set up your contracts so that you will receive payments at defined times. That way, if a client runs into a delay in the middle of a project, you still have cash flow.

- Invoice promptly. Some people recommend invoicing at the end of each month, but why wait? Invoice as soon as you've met the terms for your deliverables. Many clients prefer to wait 30 to 90 days to pay invoices, so it's better to set the clock ticking as soon as possible.

- Track your invoices. If you're happy with paper-based management of your invoices, that's no problem. However, programs like QuickBooks alert you to unpaid invoices.

But, remember, if you don't pay attention to invoice payment due dates, your clients may try to see how long they can push things. In most cases, they aren't trying to rip you off – they're simply trying to make use of your credit. If you find clients are frequently late in paying, consider charging an interest rate – and write the terms into the contract. I find this results in quick payments.

Incidentally, you don't need anything fancy to start sending out invoices. I've seen people use a word processor or spreadsheet, even for high paying contracts. You can also use basic invoicing software or opt for fancier accounting programs. It's up to you – don't feel like you have to impress anyone here. Choose an option that makes sense for you and the growth stage in which you find your business.

Notes, Thoughts and Questions about this Chapter

Things I want to consider:

Things that occurred to me:

Questions I have:

You miss 100% of the shots you don't take.

~ Wayne Gretzky

CHAPTER 14

Taking Your Best Shot

You've got the knowledge now. In this guide, you learned how to analyze your market and determine your market position before setting consulting fees. You learned to use your consulting fees as a strategic marketing tool, so that you can influence the way existing and potential clients view you and your consulting business. You also found out how to calculate a rate for your unique services – and stick to your guns when clients ask you to work for free, cut your rate or deal with annoyances. Now you're ready to actually set your consulting fees. If you follow the models and processes in this guide, you can rest assured that you've set your fees strategically, using business acumen.

Perhaps, having read this book, you feel ready to make changes immediately. You may have have an intuitive sense of what works for them and have no trouble putting thoughts into action. Or you may be the kind of person who likes to take time to have information simmer into knowledge and action – you prefer to tread carefully and with precision. That's okay too. Whatever the case, you may find that creating an action plan will help you move forward, whether today or 10 months from now.

An action plan can help turn mere ideas into reality, helping you pin down thoughts and turn them into results. With an action plan, you can get an account of the steps you need to take to bring about the goals you want to achieve.

Your plan should cover the actions, those responsible for them, deadlines and resources. Depending on the size of your organization, you may also need to work out communication and training issues and plans for dealing with any emergent issues.

In putting together an action plan, you can help yourself and your organization develop a clear picture of what needs to happen. In the case of setting consulting fees, an action plan can help you figure out what you need to do to move to a new fee model or pricing strategy. It can help you make sure you take all the details into account and get a sense of what you can accomplish in a specific period of time.

In many cases, it makes sense to roll your consulting fee action plan into your overall business plan. You will want to review your vision, mission, objectives, strategies, target market, operations, marketing and other details commonly covered in business and functional plans. For example, if you want to move to change your fees, you need to have a solid marketing plan that lends credibility to your firm. You may need to develop your sales skills or those of other people in your organization and you may need to create new sales and marketing tools, such as case studies, web content, blog posts, news releases, presentations or proposal templates. Depending on the complexity of your organization, you may need to take time to train staff, communicate new processes, hone skills and revise customer service practices and internal procedures. In some cases, you may find your business just needs a few tweaks and you're ready to roll. It all depends on you and your organization.

With that in mind, start putting together your action plan. If you are a solopreneur, you may just jot down a few tasks and deadlines and start rolling. Work with the course of action most likely to work for you. Given that Fedex was launched from Fred Smith's Yale term paper, you need not make this action plan your life's work. Just make it work for your life.

If you're not ready to move to Solution-Based Fees, that's okay. In fact, it's better to wait till you meet all the criteria on the checklist, so that you can bring power and confidence to your dealings with clients. In the meantime, if you use the models outlined in this guide, you're using proven methodologies that will help you. Quote with confidence!

Please, don't torture me with clichés. If you're going to try to intimidate me, have the courtesy to go away for a while, acquire a better education, improve your vocabulary, and come back with some fresh metaphors.

~ Dean Koontz

Glossary

Advice – an opinion, suggestion or recommendation. Professional advice is that provided by a professional with subject matter expertise.

Client – a person or organization using the professional services of an organization, including those of a sole proprietor

Consultant - professional who provides expert advice for pay

Consulting – the act of providing expert advice and professional services. May also refer to the industry.

Contact – someone with whom you have previously been in contact about your business

Contract – a written or spoken agreement creating obligations that are enforceable by law

Deposit – a partial or first payment toward a debt, such for a purchase. In consulting, the contract may indicate that the deposit will secure the vendor's time so that work can start.

Differentiation – the results of undertakings by an organization to make their offering stand out against those of the competition, with the goal of making their product look unique or better

Fee – a price charged for a service

Freelancer – an individual who provides work for hire, without commitment to a particular company or organization. May or may not providing consulting services.

Hourly rate – a rate charged by the hour

Invoice – an itemized bill

Lead – a lead is a prospective client who has passed further criteria, indicating an identifiable need, power to buy, authority to buy and an interest in hearing from you

Marketing – the activities, processes and plans related to connecting buyers and sellers, while addressing and responding to internal and external stakeholders and competitors

Maslow's Hierarchy of Needs – Abraham Maslow's description of the stages humans go through in fulfilling their needs, as published in his 1943 paper, "A Theory of Human Motivation".

Niche – a place, activity, specialization or market position for which you or your firm are suited

Niche market – a subset of a larger market

Per diem – a rate charged by the day

Prospect – a suspected potential client who has passed some initial criteria, indicating that they have good potential for become a client

Scope – the extent and details of the consulting, work or project contract

Scope creep – the evolution of consulting, work or project details to include more than was initially laid out in the project scope

Self-employment – a state of earning one's income from clients and consumers, as opposed to working for an employer

Self worth – a person's ability to see themselves as worthy, capable and valuable; dignity

SOHO (Small Office, Home Office) – a small business with 10 or fewer employees

Solution-Based Fee™ pricing– pricing using a fee charged based on the value the solution poses to the client, without specific regard for the time or costs involved in providing the solution

Spec work – short for "speculative work". Refers to work a client asks you to complete for free, with the promise that they will reimburse you if they like or use it.

Start-up – a new firm

Suspect – a potential client you suspect may need your services

SWOT – strengths, weaknesses, opportunities and threats. A managerial matrix that can help to summarize the internal and external situation for a company.

My only advice is to stay aware, listen carefully, and yell for help if you need it.

~ Judy Blume

Marketing and Business Resources

Animoto – make presentations online.
http://animoto.com/

Wordle – make word clouds.
http://www.wordle.net/

Xtranormal – turn your words into animated
video.
http://www.xtranormal.com/

Audacity – record podcasts and audio.
http://audacity.sourceforge.net/

Audioboo – record and share audio.
http://audioboo.fm/

Weebly – create a website.
http://www.weebly.com/

Edublogs – blogs for educators and facilitators.
http://edublogs.org/

Anywhere Access to Your Documents

Evernote – keep notes and documents and access
from a variety of devices.
http://evernote.com/

Dropbox – post your documents online and access from anywhere.
http://www.dropbox.com/

Google Drive
https://drive.google.com/

Microsoft Office 365
http://www.microsoft.com/en-us/office365/default.aspx

Templates and Images

iStockphoto – get inexpensive stock photos to jazz up presentations, proposals and reports.
http://www.istockphoto.com/

Microsoft Office Images – free stock photos, clip art and images.
http://office.microsoft.com/en-us/images/

Microsoft Office Templates – free templates for use with Microsoft Office software, such as Word, Excel and PowerPoint.
http://office.microsoft.com/en-us/templates/

Public & Media Relations

PRWeb – distribute news releases.
http://www.prweb.com/

Help a Reporter Out – get free publicity.
http://www.helpareporter.com/

Reference and Style Guides

Dictionary
http://dictionary.reference.com/

Thesaurus
http://thesaurus.com/

Purdue Online Writing Lab
http://owl.english.purdue.edu/

MLA
http://owl.english.purdue.edu/owl/resource/747/01/

APA
http://owl.english.purdue.edu/owl/section/2/10/

Chicago
http://owl.english.purdue.edu/owl/section/2/12/

Useit – Jakob Nielsen's Website:
http://www.useit.com/

Podcasting

iTunes Podcasting
http://www.apple.com/ca/itunes/podcasts/

Video

Youtube Creators Corner
http://www.youtube.com/t/creators_corner

Presentations

Slideshare
http://www.slideshare.net/

Presentations Magazine
http://www.presentations.com/

Inexpensive Legal Help

Law Files
http://www.lawfiles.net/

The Law
http://www.thelaw.com/

FindLaw
http://smallbusiness.findlaw.com/

Law Pivot
https://www.lawpivot.com/

Legaline (Canadian)
http://www.legalline.ca/

Canadian Bar Association (Canadian)
http://www.cba.org/bc/public_
media/lawyers/430.aspx

Right Solicitor (UK)
http://www.rightsolicitor.co.uk/

Compact Law (UK)
http://www.compactlaw.co.uk/

Aussie Legal (Australia)
http://www.aussielegal.com.au/

Referral Services

Call your local lawyer referral office and ask if they have a service where you can speak to a lawyer for free or for a short time.

Lawyers

Call a business lawyer and ask if they provide a free consultation.

Universities

Call your alumni association and ask if they provide legal benefits.

Call a law school and ask if they offer a legal clinic or drop-in service.

Community Legal Resources

Look to your local chamber of commerce and professional associations for legal information seminars.

See if your community has a Courthouse Library, access to justice society or legal services society that provides information and resources to the public.

Check your community and state for a legal information hotline.

Ask your courthouse if they have free legal services to help you represent yourself.

Teamwork is the fuel that allows common people to attain uncommon results.

~ Andrew Carnegie

Consulting Associations

Consulting associations often collect information on salaries and fees. Try contacting a professional association to find out more about typical fees for consultants. You may need to join, but even attending a meeting and chatting with other consultants may help you uncover the information you need.

General

Association of Consultants to Non-Profits
www.acnconsult.org

Association of Independent Consultants
www.aiconsult.ca

Association of Management Consulting Firms
www.amcf.org

Institute of Management Consultants (USA)
www.imcusa.org

International Council of Management
Consulting Institutes
www.icmci.org

Professional and Technical
Consultants Association
www.patca.org

Industry-Specific

Science & Technology

Association for Consultancy and Engineering
www.acenet.co.uk

Association of Consulting Chemists &
Chemical Engineers
www.chemconsult.org

Association of Consulting Engineers
www.acenet.co.uk

Chemical & Industrial Consultants Association
www.chemical-consultants.co.uk

National Association of Computer
Consultant Businesses
www.naccb.org

Security

International Association of Professional
Security Consultants
www.iapsc.org

Association of Executive Search Consultants
www.aesc.org

Association for Training & Development
www.astd.org

Human Resources Consultants Association
www.hrca.com

Healthcare

American Association of Legal
Nurse Consultants
www.aalnc.org

International Lactation Consultant Association
www.ilca.org

Business & Financial

Association of Internal Management Consultants
www.aimc.org

Consultant Industry CPAs and
Consultants Association
www.cicpac.com

International Association of Consulting Actuaries
www.actuaries.org

International Consulting Economists Association
www.icea.co.uk

Investment Management Consultants Association
www.imca.org

National Association of Real Estate Consultants
www.narec.com

Communication & Marketing

American Association of Political Consultants
www.theaapc.org

Association of Professional
Communication Consultants
www.consultingsuccess.org

Marketing Agencies Association
www.marketingagencies.org.uk/

Public Relations Consultants Association
www.prca.org.uk

Education

Higher Education Consultants Association
www.hecaonline.org

Independent Educational Consultants Association
www.educationalconsulting.org

Events

Association of Bridal Consultants
www.bridalassn.com

Association of Certified Professional
Wedding Consultants
www.acpwc.com

Miscellaneous

Association of Consultant Architects
www.acarchitects.co.uk

Association of Image Consultants International
www.aici.org

Foodservice Consultants International
www.fcsi.org

International Association of Animal
Behavior Consultants
www.iaabc.org

National Association of Legal Search Consultants
www.nalsc.org

Qualitative Research Consultants
Association www.qrca.org

Acknowledgments

They say it takes a village to raise a child. Well, it takes a village to write a book and run a business too. Thank you to my *Consultant Journal* readers for the push to put this book into print and to expand it to cover an ever increasing number of situations. And thank you to the many friends and family members who have supported me throughout 17 years of business, including seven as the editor of *Consultant Journal*. Odette Hidalgo for her never waivering support through fantastic art direction and design and countless meals. Melanie Osmack, for encouraging me to take risks and follow my heart. Sue Andrews for all the assurances about educational design and reality. Tracey Hurtado for late night calls and a safe place to fall. Lisa Manfield for countless editing tips and management of my writer's ego. Peggy Richardson for helping me get this into print at long last. Heather Workman for her years of support, right from my start in a youth entrepreneurship program through to consulting engagements and unexpected house guests.

The many good people in the MINDS entrepreneurship group, for their feedback, referrals and confidences. Elisa Hendricks for taking a risk on a young consultant, all those years ago. Joy Gugeler of Vancouver Island University for publishing advice. DeNel Sedo for her educational leadership and confidence. Maria Gomes and Maggy Kaplan for their mentorship as I took my first steps into publishing and career facilitation.

A long list of supporters, including Michele Platje-Devlin, Tess Zevenbergen, Kelly-Erin Ketchen, Jason Harrison, Yvonne Kwok, Nancy McAllister, Dee Clarke, Barbie Barter, Jovanka Connor, Shirley Weir, Katrina and Jay Forsyth, Alan and Sandy Moosmann-Patola, Anne Pepper, Vantage Point and the Hudson crew. Thanks also to Wendy W., which goes without saying. I must also thank Elizabeth Grove-White for pushing me to take risks with writing. My parents and family, for their lifelong support of my writing. My children, never last and never least, for tolerating my distractions and assurances that, if I can just answer this email, I'll be there for that concert, vacation day and school bell.

About the Author

Marketing consultant Andréa Coutu founded *Consultant Journal* (ConsultantJournal.com) a community designed to help people survive and thrive as independent consultants.

Having run Trustmode Marketing for more than 17 years, Andréa draws from experience that spans marketing and business management. Backed both by a Bachelor of Arts in English and an Executive MBA, Andréa draws from a unique blend of creative inspiration and business acumen Her marketing practice focuses on building credibility and sales for clients. She has also been a visiting professor for Simon Fraser University, taught at the University of British Columbia and published dozens of articles in magazines and newspapers. Andréa lives and works in beautiful Vancouver, Canada.

Feedback

Your feedback is valuable. I'd love to hear your thoughts. Your suggestions can help me make improvements to future versions of this guide. In fact, it's reader feedback that helped me expand the content of this book.

Please send me a note at *info@consultantjournal.com* or use the handy form at...
www.consultantjournal.com/contact.

Get 6 Tips for Jumpstarting Your Expert Status

...when you subscribe to Consultant Journal's newsletter. Written by long time consultant Andréa Coutu, the newsletter combines business tips with Andréa's real world experiences. You can unsubscribe at any time. Your email address is in good hands. And the newsletter includes actual content, not just a pitch. That explains our 5,000 +subscribers Sign up for the report at *http://consultantjournal.com/newsletter*.

Made in the USA
Lexington, KY
12 November 2015